Praise for *Get It! Street-Smart Negotiation at Work*

"Weaving entertaining and insightful yarns from his diverse experiences in the coalfields of Kentucky and corporate boardrooms across the country, Lacey Smith offers real-world advice to corporate managers who aspire to be on the fast track to success. Go get *Get It!*"

—CATHERINE FYOCK, AUTHOR,
GET THE BEST

"Probably the hardest act of persuasion is to ask men to charge into battle. *Get It!* is therefore even more of a must-read for the military, regular and reserve alike, than for almost anyone else. The best possible advice to a prospective reader: Read *Get It!* or someone else will get yours!"

—COL. WILLIAM E. PEACOCK, USMC, RET.;
FORMER ASSISTANT UNDERSECRETARY OF THE ARMY

"This book explains clearly Smith's art of persuasion and is a great read if you want to improve your negotiation skills. I learned a lot from reading it."

—ALLAN ALEXANDER, ATTORNEY AND
FORMER MAYOR OF BEVERLY HILLS, CALIFORNIA

GET IT! STREET-SMART NEGOTIATION AT WORK

GET IT!

STREET-SMART NEGOTIATION
AT WORK

How Emotions Get You What You Want

LACEY T. SMITH

Davies-Black Publishing • Mountain View, California

Published by Davies-Black Publishing, a division of CPP, Inc., 1055 Joaquin Road, Suite 200, Mountain View, CA 94043; 800-624-1765.

Special discounts on bulk quantities of Davies-Black books are available to corporations, professional associations, and other organizations. For details, contact the Director of Marketing and Sales at Davies-Black Publishing; 650-691-9123; fax 650-623-9271.

Visit the Davies-Black Publishing Web site at www.daviesblack.com.

09 08 07 06 05 10 9 8 7 6 5 4 3 2 1
Printed in the United States of America

Library of Congress Cataloging-in-Publication Data
Smith, Lacey T.
      Get it! : street-smart negotiation at work : how emotions get you what you want / Lacey T. Smith.— 1st ed.
            p. cm.
      Includes bibliographical references and index.
      ISBN 0-89106-207-6 (pbk.)
      1. Negotiation in business. 2. Emotions. I. Title.
HD58.6.S62 2005
650.1'3—dc22

                                                                             2005000515

FIRST EDITION
First printing 2005

*To Barbara Sexton Smith, my business partner and wife,
for all the usual reasons (and then some) and for founding
with me Quick Think Seminars, our teaching business,
through which thousands of our students have learned how to get it!*

CONTENTS

PART THREE: HOW THREE EMOTION-PACKED SKILLS GET IT!

FOREWORD

In the west end of Louisville where Lacey grew up, you had to be either a good fighter or a fast runner. Now, Lacey wasn't much of fighter (I see his scars every day), and he wasn't very fast. So he learned early on how to settle disputes peaceably. He learned how to negotiate. What he learned in the streets of Louisville he carried with him through his life in business, law, and politics. And now Lacey has written about these lessons for us in *Get It!*

Maybe it's because I grew up just a couple of miles from where Lacey did. Or maybe it's because I've watched him live these lessons for the twelve years we've been together, but Lacey's lessons ring true for me. I think they will for you, too.

—BARBARA SEXTON SMITH

A WORD TO THE READER

If you are like me, you've spent much of your life trying to get others to do what you want them to do. At the same time, you've been subjected to the efforts of others to get you to do what they want you to do. All this pulling and hauling can be fun. But it can be frustrating too. After all, why should it be so hard, sometimes, to get people to see it your way? Why is it that life seems so contentious?

I wrote this book to make it easier for you (and me) to understand what persuasion and negotiation are all about and to help you cut down on the contention in your life. I wrote it because as I made my way--whether in the streets, the courtrooms, the boardrooms, or the halls of government—I developed a set of working rules for negotiation, hypotheses that I routinely tested. And these hypotheses, these suppositions, have continually changed until I have arrived where I am at the end of writing this book. I kept what worked and I discarded what didn't.

At this point, to express it briefly, I believe that successful negotiations turn, not so much on numbers and analysis, but on the hopes and fears of the people involved. Negotiations are mostly about emotions and only somewhat about reason. My experience—along with some very good teachers—has brought me to this conclusion.

It would be hard to overstate the influence Harvard Law School had on my views about negotiation. Roger Fisher taught there when I was a student, and when he and Bill Ury wrote their blockbuster best-selling book, *Getting to Yes,* I went back to Cambridge to learn more about negotiation from them. I also learned a lot about negotiation living with my five law school roommates there on Concord Avenue. They always designated me the chief negotiator with our landlord, a first-generation Italian American. He and I drank a lot of Chianti at the bargaining table.

Max Bazerman at Northwestern's Kellogg School was another of my teachers. His book *Negotiating Rationally* also had a strong influence on my views about successful negotiations, especially the section about common mistakes.

These teachers, along with some others, taught me principles of negotiation. But I was a skeptical student. I tested what they taught against what I experienced. As an attorney, I negotiated for the city of Louisville's cable franchise agreement. I was a special counsel for the Commonwealth of Kentucky in negotiating with the Nixon administration regarding health care regulations.

As a state senator and chairman of the education committee, I negotiated to bring the University of Louisville, which had been a private institution, into public higher education on an equal financial footing with the other state schools. As an entrepreneur in the health care, food service, dry-cleaning, and coal businesses I negotiated with lenders, government agencies, health care network officials, employees, and customers.

In these varied settings, public and private, I tested the hypotheses about negotiation I had been taught. This book is a culmination of these teachings, shaped by my experience. For you, it is an easy book to grasp.

Part One shows you how emotions determine who *gets it*. Part Two demonstrates how you should prepare in your negotiations to *get it*. Part Three introduces you to three emotion-packed skills to help you *get it*: empathy, rapport, and baking a bigger pie (so you get a bigger piece). The last chapter recaps five lessons from the street, of the sixty-five in the book, that you'll want to remember.

As you read the stories in this book, please know that they all happened. I didn't make them up. I did, however, make up some of the names of the people involved to protect their privacy; but otherwise you can count on my experiences as the real ones from which I draw my conclusions about how you can *get it*.

Enjoy the book, and I hope to see you sometime out there in the streets, negotiating!

ABOUT THE AUTHOR

Lacey T. Smith grew up in the Portland section of Louisville, Kentucky. His mother was the head of the household; she drove a Checker taxicab at night while Lacey ran the streets, not always one step ahead of the authorities. Many of his friends spent some time in prison (one died there); but, mostly because of a teacher who played viola in the Louisville Orchestra—and showed him a world beyond the streets—Lacey emerged from Portland with not enough scars to keep him from graduating from Princeton University's Woodrow Wilson School of Public and International Affairs where he was the founding editor of the journal *Public and International Affairs,* and from the Harvard Law School. While at Harvard, he taught economics at Brandeis University.

Lacey has worked as a reporter for the *Louisville Times* and the *Minneapolis Tribune* (now the *Star Tribune*). He also has served as an assistant attorney general for the Commonwealth of Kentucky and was twice elected to the Kentucky state senate, where he was chairman of the education committee. As a senator, he was elected by the capital press corps as "Outstanding Senator in the Public Interest" and, twice, "Outstanding Orator in the Senate."

Lacey has taught as well at the University of Louisville and as an adjunct professor in the MBA program at Bellarmine University where he created courses in negotiation skills and in new venture creation. While at Bellarmine, he won the Metroversity Award for Excellence in Teaching.

More than an academician, Lacey has created, developed, and sold several businesses with hundreds of employees and millions of dollars in
sales in the health care industry, the coal business, and the restaurant and
dry-cleaning businesses. He and his wife, Barbara Sexton Smith, an Ernst
& Young Entrepreneur of the Year nominee, teach negotiation strategies
and tactics to managers of domestic and international business concerns.

HOW EMOTIONS DETERMINE WHO GETS IT!

GET WHAT YOU WANT

The Role of Emotions in Whether You Get It!

Most of the time your emotions—your hopes and fears—not your reason, determine what you say, what you do, and what you get from all your interactions from other people. The results of these interactions—many of them efforts to persuade—turn, not on numbers and analysis, but on these hopes and fears.

This is no reason for despair. Emotions and feelings can lead us to excellent results.

It may not be easy to accept this view. Most of us believe that emotion and reason are at war within ourselves, and smart money bets on reason. It's got a better reputation, is associated with the mind, and is more elegant, less messy—especially in matters of business and commerce—than feelings, which have traditionally been associated with the body and are sometimes out of control. But reputation and elegance alone do not have the raw power of the visceral. Besides, as we shall see, there is no war. The mind and the body are not two disconnected compartments for our reason and our feelings. Reason and feelings do not have to diminish each other.

On the contrary, as professor Antonio Damasio has demonstrated from his work with brain-damaged patients and reported in *Looking for Spinoza,*[1] reason and feelings can and do support and enrich one another. They are inextricably connected. And this is good for results in all life's negotiations.

Hopes and fears, in concert with our feeling brains, are the major emotions that drive us and help us or prevent us from getting what we want.

Hopes from Experience . . .
High Hopes from Confidence and Trust

We hear a lot about hope: Hope springs eternal in the human breast (Alexander Pope). While there's life, there's hope (Cicero). Hope built this country, not cynicism (Senator John Edwards).[2]

But what is hope? Try this. Hope is the belief that something wonderful can happen because we remember a similar experience that was wonderful. Something wonderful, in other words, can happen again. From the tee, we drive our ball to the apron of the green. This could happen again, so we play on, though we muff one shot after another.

We persist. Not because of a triumph of hope *over* experience, as Dr. Samuel Johnson claimed, observing a man marry immediately on the death of his first wife, with whom he had been miserable. No. What sustains us is the triumph of hope *because of* experience. In our memories we tend to accentuate the positive and eliminate the negative.

HIGH HOPES

What about high hopes? Hopes that go beyond wonderful and cross over into dreams of the superlative? These are what I call "para-experience" hopes—hopes not undergirded by a similar experience but growing out of confidence in ourselves and/or, perhaps, trust in something bigger than ourselves.

Some of you may remember the story about the ant that believed he could move a rubber tree plant or the ram that thought he could punch a hole in a dam. No proof is offered that either had done it before, but they didn't know they couldn't do it.

FALSE HOPES

Now, some will say that high hopes are dangerous. They point to the theory of psychoanalyst Karen Horney and her Idealization-Frustration-Demoralization hypothesis.[3] Some will say, in other words, that high hopes are false hopes whose illusions frustrate us and, in time, demoralize us.

In a way, however, in the sense that everything hoped for contains the possibility of not materializing—in that sense—all hope is false.

But if hope lifts us up and helps us take productive action we might not otherwise take, why attach a pejorative meaning to it? Why call it false?

I'll stand with the ant and the ram regardless of the odds. I may not have guaranteed success, but going forward anyway is worth a shot.

Our hopes, our ambitions, our goals, our dreams can sustain us in the face of overwhelming odds, against great adversity. Not logic. Not reason. Not our brains alone. But rather it is our hearts and the hopes in them that buoy us up and carry us on.

STREET-SMART REALITY
HOPE, A PRECURSOR TO ACTION

The rock climber had hope that he could scale the walls of a difficult canyon. He had done it before, and this memory gave him belief in his chances for success. When his arm became trapped by the sudden shifting of a half-ton boulder, he believed he could work his way out. He'd been in tight spots before. But unable to move after great effort, and not wanting to stay there and die, he cut his arm off at the elbow with the hope, the high hope, that he could remain conscious, not bleed to death, and climb back to safety and to civilization. His brain told him what to do. His heart told him he could do it. So he did it and then walked six miles to get medical treatment.

> **LESSON FROM THE STREET #1**
>
> Hope frees you from fear.

Or maybe it happened in reverse. Maybe his heart led him to believe he could do what was necessary to extricate himself from his trap; and with that belief and with his mind freed from the freeze of fear, he was able to think his way out of his predicament.

———

Hope also shapes and defines much of our efforts to persuade others.

STREET–SMART REALITY
CONFIDENCE, ANOTHER FACE OF HOPE

Evangelista was upbeat as she prepared for her annual evaluation. A big raise was in the offing. More job responsibility. A corner office. Less travel.

> ### LESSON FROM THE STREET #2
>
> In persuasion, keep your hopes high. You won't do better than your highest hopes.

More time to be with her seven- and nine-year-old children. Less friction between her and her husband, a stay-at-home dad. She had scored well in quarterly evaluations, and she had a great relationship with her boss of nearly four years. She had concerns, of course. Kim was up for the same job, but Kim had less time in the position, was younger, and didn't enjoy such a good working relationship with the boss.

All in all, Evangelista was full of hope as she walked to the conference room. She was confident she could persuade her boss to give her what she wanted and deserved. As she walked, she softly whistled a happy tune so no one (most of all herself) would suspect she was—yes—a little bit afraid.

What's your prediction about Evangelista and her hopes, her aspirations, her expectations?

She's likely to persuade her boss, isn't she? She will probably translate her dreams into reality based on her past job performance and a good evaluation interview.

As New York Jets' Joe Namath, better known for his football feats and philandering than for philosophy, once said: "If you don't dream it, it won't happen."[4]

———

Hopes can be high and higher, and they impact what happens in our interactions with our co-workers.

NOTHING IS BETTER THAN SOMETHING

Other factors from our education and our culture can also affect what we feel as we attempt to persuade others.

STREET-SMART REALITY
FAIRNESS AND LOGIC

One of my professors told the story of the eccentric, wealthy man who offered a $100 bill to two strangers on the street under the condition that one of the strangers would decide how to divide the money between the two, but the second would have to agree to that division or neither would get anything. Time after time, in offers to pairs of strangers, if the first (the divider), gave less than 50 percent to the second (the decider), the deal would be rejected.

The professor's lesson: Americans, at least, have a concept of what is fair, and they tend to believe that if they don't come out as well as the other side, they don't like the deal. Even if you walk away with, say, $25—$25 more than you had before the wealthy man made his offer—you don't consider it fair, because the person proposing the division gets more than you.

I decided to test the lesson with a crisp $100 bill I took to the street. It's not easy to give away money in our country. Most people didn't want to participate. Those who gave a reason feared a scam.

When I got two takers, the proposed division was 50-50, but it was rejected. I was stunned and so was the woman who proposed the division.

The explanation? "She should have reasoned that giving me more would have guaranteed I would take the deal."

The rejecter (decider) had an interesting perspective, but the point is the same. Rejecting the deal was an emotional, not a rational, decision because the rejecter walked without the $50 he could have had for no more effort than saying yes.

> **LESSON FROM THE STREET #3**
>
> What's "fair" most often determines who gets what, and what's fair is often not logical.

In ten years of teaching negotiation, we have simulated this exercise on scores of occasions, and about 85 percent of the time the proposed division is 50-50 and it is accepted. When the divider takes more for himself, most of the time the deal is rejected. The explanation is always the same: "It's unfair."

Someone invariably points out that something is better than nothing, but this changes few minds.

Once in a seminar at General Electric there were eight Mexican participants from the MABE joint venture near Mexico City, and the five who were deciders each gave more than $50 to the second participant. Their explanations were similar: They feared that even a 50-50 split could lose the deal. They wanted a lock. The man in the street who rejected the 50-50 split of my $100 would have liked these offers.

Hopes, fears, cultural norms of fairness—feelings—triumph repeatedly over pure logic in this negotiation exercise.

My own experience in actual negotiations carried on in a wide range of circumstances—in politics, in business, in community service, and (of course) in personal matters—indicates that, as in our seminars, emotions shape the contours of what happens as we try to *get it!*

Fears That Someone Else Will Do Well . . .
Fears That We Will Be Hurt by Something We Do

If you grow up in Kentucky, you will develop, somewhere along the line, the ambition to be governor and/or a coal baron. I never made it to governor, though I did become a state senator. In the coal business I became something less than a baron—maybe a baronet. And while the money I made in coal was not beyond the dreams of avarice, I did gain some valuable knowledge in the coalfields about how emotions affect the outcomes of negotiations.

STREET-SMART REALITY
VARIATION ON THE DOG-IN-THE-MANGER STORY

Early on during my days in the western Kentucky coalfields, I worked very hard to sell coal to the GAF corporation located in Calvert City, Kentucky. The GAF plant there required a special size of coal, 0.75-by-0.25 inches, and crushing it to that size caused more than 50 percent of a ton to be too small for GAF to use. Something else had to be done with these "fines," because the coal producers couldn't afford to waste them. If they had an order from a big utility, such as the Tennessee Valley Authority, which could use coal that small, there was no problem. But most operators didn't have such contracts, so the GAF order was hard to fill.

At this point in my coal career, I was a broker. I dug no coal of my own. But a friend from my Jaycee days was in business with two others from Louisville. They were digging coal in western Kentucky, and they had an order from a utility that could take fines.

Opal Lee, an accountant by trade, had traded her Ferragamo pumps for the black, steel-toed boots we all wore in the coalfields, and the day I visited her she had them propped up on her green metal, government-issue desk. She had so adopted the coalfield culture, I half expected her to take a chaw out of a plug of Red Man tobacco and start spittin' in a Styrofoam cup. She didn't do that, but she and her partners had signed a couple of fairly big contracts recently, and she was, as we say in Kentucky, "big feelin'."

After respectfully listening to stories of how she became a major mogul, I quoted her a price on my deal, which included two dollars a ton for me on a 3,000-ton-a-month order. The price to her, minus my fee, was quite attractive, and we agreed she would put the paperwork together and conduct a test burn the following week. GAF would pay her, and she would pay me.

When I returned to Madisonville the following week, Opal Lee had changed her mind. After some hemming and hawing, she reluctantly admitted that although the price to her was excellent, and although I had added value to the deal (I had worked for nearly a year to get the order), she didn't want to do it.

"Lacey, it's going to gall me to write you a check for $6,000 every month."

"Get somebody else to write the check, or I'll handle the money and pay you," I said.

She wouldn't budge.

"Opal Lee, you're worse than the dog in the manger who couldn't eat the hay but wouldn't let the cow eat it either. I'm giving you some good hay you can eat, but you won't take it because I'll get some too."

But she had made up her mind. Or, I should say, her feelings had made up her mind for her. Logic said we should make the deal, but Opal Lee's

LESSON FROM THE STREET #4

Sometimes people won't do what's good for them if they think it is "too" good for you.

feelings said otherwise. Her feelings, though, helped me dodge a bullet, because she and her partners went out of business later that year. And I found someone who was not galled by writing me that $6,000 check every month.

Looking back, I concluded that when I approached her, times were too flush for my friend, and the prospect of profits was not as positive a feeling as the negative feelings she conjured up at the thought of paying me as "merely" a broker in the deal.

———

At first, I chalked up the experience with Opal Lee as an aberration. To be sure, I had observed on many occasions how emotions lead people down a path away from what would seem to be their best interests. I had seen greed, ego, sex, and the love of power lead politicians to self-destruction. But I considered politicians somehow a breed apart, possessed of different DNA than the rest of the population. In time, however, I came to believe that the way emotions determined what happened in Madisonville that day was not a deviation from the norm. It was squarely astride the norm.

What happened to me in Florida helped bring me to that conclusion.

STREET–SMART REALITY
PERCEPTIONS AND EMOTIONS

The church I attended when I lived in southern Florida in the 1990s was booming. In a rapidly growing part of a rapidly growing state, it had 9,000 members. It was my church. Luther Mansfield, its pastor, had baptized me. Although young and energetic, Luther was also a tired and troubled man. The growth of his church was wearing him down. For one thing, he was forced by the size of his sanctuary to conduct multiple services on Sunday morning and another service Sunday evening. Although the church had money for construction, there was no room to expand, because the building was bounded on every side but one by highways and waterways. On its west border, however, was a complex of thirty-six garden-style apartments on nearly two acres. I owned this property, and thereby hangs a tale.

Wishing to sell the apartments and desirous of doing well by doing good, I made a proposal to the church that was classically too good to refuse.

The property appraised at $3.2 million, and it had a mortgage on it for $1.6 million. At 95 percent occupancy, the apartments were producing about $50,000 a year.

I proposed selling the property to the church for the appraised value, payable by the assumption of the mortgage and a five-year no-interest note in my favor for $1.6 million. During the sixty months of the note, I pledged to Luther and to Fred, head of the church development committee, that I would help them find a donor for the $1.6 million balance. If we could not find a donor, I promised to take the property back, and the church would earn $250,000 during the search period.

> **LESSON FROM THE STREET #5**
>
> Don't assume your perception of what is good for others is their perception. They may have different information, different emotions.

Luther and Fred's enthusiasm for my idea cannot be exaggerated—especially Luther's, who saw in the proposal much-needed relief from his backbreaking schedule.

The development committee of the church, however, flatly turned the deal down.

"Some of the folks on the committee were afraid of the liability of operating an apartment complex and of being responsible for the people who lived there," Fred reported.

"That's why there is insurance," I said. "Plus, you could fill the apartments with only your best-behaved parishioners."

Their feelings were firm, however, and I sold the apartments to another buyer. The church was not expanded. And Luther Mansfield left to pastor a church in another state with a bigger sanctuary. One of the last things he said to me was, "Lacey, where there is no vision, the people perish."

Again, at first, as with the GAF coal deal, I put the church's decision down to aberrant behavior. But I was wrong. Like Opal Lee, the church committee in Florida merely had a different perspective from mine. Their perspective was shaped by *their fears* about what negative things could happen if they owned an apartment complex, not what positive benefits there would be for the church to have this extra land (to say nothing about the fact that I was going to help them find someone to pay for it).

———

Through the rosy lens of retrospect, I could have done things that may have made a difference in both western Kentucky and in Florida.

First, in the coal deal, I should have foreseen that when Opal Lee knew how much money I was making, she may have had a bad reaction—even though she was getting exactly what she wanted. But I wanted to do what was easiest. That is, Opal Lee was set up to bill GAF and handle the accounting, and letting her take care of the mechanics was easiest, but obviously not best, for getting the deal done. Putting Opal Lee between me and GAF was not a good idea in any case. It gave her too much opportunity to interfere with my relationship with them. It was fortunate that she turned me down.

Second, as I have replayed (many times) my offer to the church, I realize that I could have done what I said I would do: to wit, find them a donor for the balance. But I could keep the property in my name until we found that donor. The only difficulty with that scenario is that at the time I wished to return to Kentucky, and the property was too small for absentee ownership. I would have had to stay in Florida to manage it.

So, feelings, fears, emotions—that's what determined the outcome of the church negotiation, as well as Opal Lee's decision in the Kentucky coalfields.

These conclusions are not unique to my experience. And, of course, there are subtle variations on these conclusions.

Fears of Loss Versus Hope for Gain . . . Discomfort and Framing

Daniel Kahneman and Amos Tversky, prize-winning social scientists, have demonstrated that even in making dollars-and-cents decisions, decisions that directly affect our pocketbooks, we are guided more by fear of loss than by reason.[5]

Conduct this experiment. The next time you are with a group of friends, offer to bet with them on the toss of a coin. Make this proposal: "I'm going to toss this coin and you may call heads or tails. If you choose wrong, you lose $10. How much would you need to win by choosing correctly to be willing to make this bet?"

Irrespective of the economic circumstances of your friends, you will find, as Kahneman and Tversky did, that most of those who are willing to bet will require an upside of more than $10, some as much as $30, to make the bet.

Now, logic would indicate that a possible gain of $10 is what would be required to make the bet, since the odds are 50-50 that you will win the toss. But logic doesn't tip the balance. Emotions do. Why is this? And what are the broader implications of this phenomenon for you as you try to get it?

Niccolo Machiavelli, who wrote *The Prince,* didn't conduct any blind studies or other social scientific research. But he was a close observer of his fellow citizens in fifteenth-century Florence. He anticipated Kahneman and Tversky in concluding that a leader could do better with his followers if they were motivated more by fear than by love. Of course the best leaders are, because of brilliance and circumstance (Alexander the Great, for example, and Henry V—at least Shakespeare's version) at once feared and loved. But such leaders are rare.

Twentieth-century economist Ludwig Von Mises, less Darwinian than Machiavelli but no less on target about human action, concluded that man won't move without being spurred on by discomfort. The prospect of something better is not sufficient if the status quo is acceptable. There has to be that burr under the saddle to make the horse of human nature giddyup.[6]

One possible implication of this emotion-based process is that in making a proposal, you should frame it in terms of the ill that will befall those who refuse to accede to your request rather than the great things that will follow if they do. Of course, these potentially dire results have to be presented tactfully.

"John, I know you could make this deal with Impact Technology Co., but take a look at their recent SEC filings. They are headed down a different road, and I predict that a year from now they won't be as good a match for you as we will be, and, if you go with them, you could be quite disappointed."

Or, in making a proposal for a contract renewal, for example, cast your expressions, if possible, in terms of the benefits of the proposal compared with the current deal and not in terms that are in response to the other side's proposed changes to the current deal.

LESSON FROM THE STREET #6

People are motivated more by fear of loss than by the hope for gain.

Any proposition that the other side sees as less than they proposed, they will see as a loss, and you will meet stiff resistance. But if your proposal can be framed as a gain from the current contract, even if that gain takes both sides to exactly the same place as the response to their proposal, it will be more palatable.

People will act to avoid what they consider a loss.

In the workplace, as in your personal life, the contours and outcomes of persuasions and negotiations are shaped, not so much by numbers and analysis, elegant proofs, and rigorous demonstrations. Instead, they are shaped for the most part by the emotions—the hopes and fears—of those involved. It's your job to identify these hopes and fears—yours and those on the other side if you are to *get it.*

2

UNCOVER EMOTIONS TO REVEAL REAL INTERESTS

Two Reasons for Everything— the One You Give and the Real Reason

There are two reasons for everything: the one you give and the real reason.

This is not a bad assumption under which to operate. Nor is this just a cynical expression. It's not that people always hide their real interests, though they may. Sometimes people have not figured out the real reason they need or want something. You're not sure what you want, and the folks on the other side aren't sure what they want either.

Part of the reason for this lack of clarity is that many times we have mixed motives. We ask for a raise at work at the same time we ask for a lighter travel schedule. We want a solid marriage, but we pursue a life better suited to singles.

Plus, we are not always fully conscious of all our feelings about a particular matter. How many times, for example, have you become aware— perhaps because of some physical expression like tapping your fingers on the steering wheel of your car—that you feel anxious? You have been feeling this way for some time, but you have just now become aware of it.

Your anxiety didn't come on you like a sneeze. But there it is—soon followed by the emotions it engenders.

Unpacking these emotions so we can get at the real reasons behind our positions—the things we say we want and that we will and won't do—can get complicated.

The Things We Say . . .
Why We Say Them

Your job, if you are going to get most of what you want most of the time, is to figure out what your real feelings are about what is at stake as well as the real feelings of the people with whom you are dealing—in other words, the people on your side and the people on the other side.

You want $210,000 for your house? All right, but why? The $210,000 is what you say you want, but what are the feelings that led you to that number? Is it the price you paid times the consumer price index compounded for the five years you have lived there, and this seems fair? Is it the price your spouse says you have to have or he won't sign the papers? Is $210,000 higher than market because you love the house, and that is what a buyer will have to come up with to take it from you? Or have you set the price lower than market because you want a quick sale so you can meet the required closing date on your new house, and you can't afford two house payments?

To be successful in getting what you want, it is important for you to understand what feelings shape what you say you want and what you say you will or won't do. This is true in your professional as well as your personal life.

If, for example, you are committed to your company's mission statement, is what you do day to day to advance your career consistent with that commitment? Or is there a divergence? In other words, are your personal goals in line with those of your department, your company? Sorting through questions like these and their answers is an important prologue to any successful business transaction that turns on persuasion.

STREET-SMART REALITY
YOU—THE LAST PERSON YOU WANT TO FOOL!

Penny had worked for five years at a major insurance company as a financial analyst. One acquisition after another had created a corporate organization with four business units and four distinct sets of operating statements each month.

Management decided to consolidate its financial results into one monthly report and accordingly pulled together an ad hoc team of more than twenty employees from across the company to choose a provider for the design of a new general ledger and income statement and then to assist in its installation. The ad hoc team would work nearly full-time for a year to do this, and Penny was asked to serve on the team.

In the beginning Penny was enthusiastic about the new assignment. She made suggestions, attended every meeting, volunteered to chair an important subcommittee, and began to emerge as a real leader. She devoted full time to her role.

A few months passed and rumors began to float around about the possible sale of the company. Not long after the rumors surfaced, Penny's behavior changed. Her attendance became spotty. She didn't call meetings of her subcommittee. She spent less and less time on the general ledger project and more and more time at the tasks of her regular job.

The team chairman complained to Penny's supervisor, Lupe, who asked her what was wrong.

"My work is suffering because of the general ledger project."

"I'll get you help."

"Then I'll have to spend time training that help, and that will take even more time."

Lupe helped Penny review her current job load to see which tasks could be put off pending the completion of the ad hoc project.

"We'll put these on hold until the project is completed," Lupe concluded.

Still, Penny's motivation did not improve.

Sean, a consultant known for his perceptiveness and caring, had been brought in to build the ad hoc committee into a team. He began meeting with Penny. After a number of conversations, Penny admitted to Sean, but most importantly to herself, that the reason for her declining enthusiasm about the general ledger project was that she feared if the company were sold and she had spent all this time on a project that could have little meaning to a new owner, her regular job might disappear or be filled by someone else.

Penny began to be a better team member only after she received assurances from Lupe's superior that her job, irrespective of her absence, was not in jeopardy.

Months later Penny admitted that her growing sense of anxiety about her job, the demands of the team project, and the rumors about the sale of the company did not become focused for her until the consultant began coaching her.

"I was kidding myself about what was really bothering me," she remembered.

Don't fool yourself. When you are feeling some unfocused anxiety about issues at work, do Exercise 1.

If figuring out what is motivating you is tough, it is sometimes double tough to figure out what is going on with those on the other side of an issue.

What Others Say ...
What They Mean

We begin our lives as screaming masses of protoplasm, totally centered on ourselves, crying for food, for dry diapers, for love and affection. It takes most of us a lifetime to get outside ourselves and become genuinely empathic to the feelings of others. Some of us never make much progress in the empathy department. But for each of us, it is difficult to move across the table and sit in the chair of our opposer. Those who are able to do this best, in my experience, are the best negotiators. They get what they want most often.

Exercise 1

YOUR DOMINANT EMOTIONS

Answer the following six questions.

Why am I meeting and talking with these people (on my side and on the other side)?

_____

What do I hope to accomplish?

_____

What does my boss want me to accomplish?

_____

What is at stake for me personally?

_____

What hopes do I have in connection with any likely outcome?

_____

What fears or concerns do I have in connection with a worst-case outcome?

_____

Now, take an inventory of your answers. When your answers to two or more questions are the same, you have uncovered at least some of the dominant emotions shaping the positions you take as you try to persuade someone.

It may seem counterintuitive to focus on others to get what you want. But solving the problems of the other side can go a long way toward solving your own problems.

Remember the *Jerry Maguire* movie with Tom Cruise and Cuba Gooding Jr.? Well, even if you didn't see it, you've probably heard the line that Gooding's character made famous: "Show me the money!"[1]

Cruise, for our purposes, delivers an even better line to his football player client, Rod Tidwell, played by Gooding. Tidwell emerges naked from the Arizona Cardinal locker room and confronts Cruise about his contract and demands that Cruise, in effect, show him the money. Cruise responds,

"Rod, you don't know what it's like being *me* out here trying to help *you*. I need help. Help me. Rod, help me! You've got to help *me* help *you!* Help *me* help *you!*"

This is a plea that others should not have to make to you. You should help them on your own initiative. Not because of altruism. Not because you are good person. Not because you've read somewhere that every conflict should end up as a win-win deal. No. You should try to help the other side solve its problem because it is in your best interest to do so.

I'm not talking here about trying to "save" someone on the other side of a negotiation so you can preserve your relationship for a better, brighter day in the future. I'm not talking about taking a hit yourself because someone made a bad deal, underestimated a cost, or wants you to share the burden of his mistake. No. You help people solve their problems so you can, thereby, find a way to advance your full set of interests.

STREET-SMART REALITY

HELP OTHERS HELP YOU

The owners of a small logistics company, Preliminary, had been negotiating to sell the company to Huge Services, a larger firm in the same field, and the negotiations dragged on. The larger company kept identifying things it needed to make a decision: explanations of certain entries on the financial statements, a complete tagged list of every hard asset of the smaller company, interviews with key employees, assurances from certain major customers, endless back-and-forth between the lawyers on legal points of the documents.

At last, at a meeting both sides characterized as "final," the Huge Services people presented a list of things they needed before going to contract. There were seven items. They involved matters such as rent abatements, escalators for the leases, structured commissions on a business earn-out, a four- to six-week "kick-out" period during which, after the execution of documents, the buyers could walk for any reason they deemed sufficient. Each item was discussed at length.

LESSON FROM THE STREET #8

Focus on the problems of the other guy. You'll go a long way toward solving yours.

During a time-out, a member of Preliminary said, "Why should we give them four to six weeks to come in here and kick our tires, talk to our customers, find out everything about us and then walk? If they are afraid we know something they don't, that's their problem."

The chief financial officer said, "That may be their problem, but if we don't find a way to help them solve it, we won't have a deal. And that will be our problem."

The two sides resumed the negotiation. The Preliminary CFO made a long-shot suggestion:

"Look, you've given us a list of seven things you want. Help us out. Tell us which are most important."

In response, and somewhat to the Preliminary team's surprise, the president of Huge listed the seven items in the order of their importance to them—top to bottom—one through seven.

After another time out, Preliminary was able to propose a solution that took each side's interests into account, advancing its full set of interests and meeting Huge's interests—especially the number one concern—in an acceptable manner. It was a done deal.

Consider this: If you could read the minds of the persons across the bargaining table, you would have a significant advantage, would you not? The advantage, though, would not arise merely because you would know what they had been purposely keeping from you—their reservation price, or what they would do if you don't reach agreement. This information would, of course, be of incalculable value to you. Your real advantage, though, would be that you would know their fondest hopes and worst fears. With the knowledge of their feelings, you would know what to say and do and how to say and do it to maximize the likelihood of their saying yes to what you are asking of them.

Does this make sense?

That's what happened with the logistics company sale. The buyer was led by questions into prioritizing its requests, and, with this information, the seller was able to help the buyer get what it needed most. As a consequence, the seller was able to get what it needed most—the deal.

But how do you get inside the heads and the hearts of those on the other side to help them? How do you learn the difference between the reasons they give and the real ones, between what is said and what is meant?

Those on the other side will tell you the difference between what they say and what they mean. And why will they do this? Because you lead them to realize that to get what *they want,* they have to *help you help them.* They can do this only by sharing what they feel about what the issues are between you.

Your task is to lead them to this realization. You do this with questions. And of the world of questions, there is no end.

QUESTIONS OF CONNECTION

Where I come from and live now, one of the first things people seem to ask each other when they meet is "Where did you go to high school?"

This is a kind of touchstone to see what kind of bond or connection may be established so the rapport-building process can begin. Once a connection is made—they competed on the football field or dated someone from the other school—folks no longer look on each other as strangers. They begin to open up to one another.

Can so small a connection make a difference? Absolutely. In fact, the more connections you can make by asking questions about earlier times in the person's life, the more you will become, not a new friend, but like an old one. And the more they will open up to you.

In these matters, as may be expected, sincerity of expression is important. Feigned emotional connections and insincere questions are easily detected and produce results opposite of what you want. They are, to paraphrase Shakespeare, like a painting of emotion: a face without a heart.

"WHY" AND "WHY NOT" QUESTIONS

"Where did you go to high school?" is only one of the many questions that help you uncover the hopes and fears of the people with whom you are dealing. "Why" is a key question, but I've found that many times people are reluctant to answer "why" questions.

"Why do we want that much to do the job? Because that's our standard fee."

Often, however, people who will not answer a "why" question will answer a question like "What is wrong with . . . ?" or "Why wouldn't this work . . . ?"

"I'll tell you why that won't work: This is wrong, and that is wrong, and also this other thing is wrong, too."

"Well, what if instead we did A, B, and C?"

"I'll tell you what is wrong with *that*."

People like to be critics and tell you what is wrong with your idea or proposal without telling you what their idea, belief, prejudice, hope, or concern is. As they tell you everything that is wrong with your proposal, you can begin to infer what may be acceptable to them—what their proposal would look like if they would just be straightforward about it.

As they tell you what is wrong with what you are saying, keep posing hypotheticals, and let them continue to respond with their critiques until their negatives become pregnant with what is in their hearts and minds—until, that is, you begin to understand what hopes and fears are dictating their positions.

Sometimes asking questions to uncover real feelings is a tricky process. Tact is a great quality to possess at times like these. So is empathy and, of course, rapport. Inventiveness and creativity are pluses as well.

CREATIVE QUESTIONS

In the movie *All the President's Men,* about the Watergate affair, Carl Bernstein of the *Washington Post* tries at one point to persuade a staff person from the Committee to Reelect the President to reveal the names of the three men who had access to the millions of dollars in the reelection fund. She declines to say and won't budge. Finally, Dustin Hoffman, playing Bernstein, suggests a way to provide the information without giving the actual names.

"I'll give you an initial, and if the name does not begin with that initial, shake your head. If it does, nod your head," he said.

There were a limited number of people who could have had access to the fund, so Bernstein got his information, and the staffer didn't, technically at least, divulge the names. She could never be identified as a source. It was a delicate dance orchestrated by creative questions.[2]

ELLIPTICAL QUESTIONS

Back in your grammar school days (you probably called them grade school days), you may have learned about elliptical sentences—sentences from which something was intentionally deleted and the omission was marked by ellipses, as in "John was a real . . . but his friends overlooked that quality."

One of the most effective forms of questions to get inside the heads of those with whom you deal is what I call the elliptical question. I first became aware of this type of question when I was a reporter for the *Minneapolis Tribune* (now the *Star Tribune*).

STREET-SMART REALITY
CREATE A PAUSE IN THE RIGHT PLACE

David Mazie was a young reporter also working there at the time. I had just come on the paper and one of my first assignments was to accompany Dave on a story involving the crash of a small plane as it landed at the airport. The FAA had not begun its investigation, and everyone involved was reluctant to answer any questions or go on record about anything.

But Dave uncovered the essential information with his elliptical questions.

"When you first saw the plane on the radar screen was it already in trouble, or . . . ?"

The first part of his question called for a yes or no answer, but the "or" followed by a pause pressured the target of his question to fill in the blank and not duck out with just a one-word answer, if he were at all inclined to be expansive.

"It didn't seem to be in trouble when I first saw it, but within a few minutes we heard the pilot say something that made us think he was."

"And . . . ?"

"Well, he didn't say anything to the tower directly, but he seemed to be talking to himself."

"Was he in an agitated state, or . . . ?"

And so it went. Dave would offer a few words suggesting the subject of the question and then a conjunction or disjunction followed by an elliptical pause. The witnesses filled in the elliptical spaces.

We got the story.

———

Most people are uncomfortable with silence. An elliptical question with its unsaid words hanging in the air creates silence, and this produces, as often as not, awkwardness. People respond to remove the awkwardness. The elliptical question is a good technique when folks on the other side are playing their cards close to their vests.

QUESTIONS OF CLARIFICATION

If you ask a group of employees to identify the major problem at work, invariably among the top three issues will be the problem of communication.

A consultant separately asked the top twelve managers of a large company to share the mission statement of the company. He got twelve versions. When this divergence of opinion was reported to the CEO, he said, with anger, "I shouldn't have to hammer into the heads of people making more than $200,000 a year what our mission is!"

"Well, maybe you shouldn't have to, but if you want them to have a common understanding of the mission, you're going to have to."

When this same consultant asked an employee working on the production line how what he was doing fit into the company's mission statement, the employee looked as if the consultant had spoken to him in Chinese.

If you are trying to persuade someone to a point of view, ask them at various points, "Does what I am saying make sense?" Or, "Can you use these services I am describing?" "Does this seem fair?"

Alternatively, if someone has made a proposal to you and you are considering a response, before you respond, seek clarification: "Tunica, let me see if I understand what you are saying."

LESSON FROM THE STREET #10

In communication, there's no such thing as too much clarification.

Repeat what she has said in your words. Then, give her a chance to verify that you understand her.

Questions of clarification can let you know whether you are on the right track. And they give the other side a chance to set you straight. People like to do that.

QUESTIONS ANTICIPATING OBJECTIONS

Hardee's hamburger chain, in an effort to bolster flagging same-store sales, undertook in early 2003 a unique advertising campaign. The ads purported to be interviews with customers who began by offering a criticism of Hardee's.[3]

"My mom can cook fried chicken, mashed potatoes, gravy, and greens, and she can cook 'em just about better'n anybody. So, Hardee's, why don't you just stick to makin' hamburgers?"

That's right, you say. Just what you've been thinking. Stick to hamburgers. If they'll do that, then I'll hurry on over to Hardee's the way I used to do. You've anticipated my objection and met it with a question raised by a believable customer. Hardee's did a good job presenting the negative to get the positive response.

STREET-SMART REALITY
CONFRONT THE NEGATIVE, GET A POSITIVE

The best question I ever heard anticipating an objection and quelling it was in a little town in Oklahoma.

After my baronet experience in the coal business, I was just arrogant enough to think I could strike it rich in the oil business. Coal . . . oil. Both black. Both commodities. Similar business models. This won't be that hard, I reasoned, if I can just find me a mentor. Jim Smith was my mentor in the coal business. I needed one for oil.

I knew just the man to see. Vaughn Good. I'd met Vaughn at the Kentucky Derby and had spoken with him at length about his home state of Oklahoma and his oil business. He said if I ever wanted to see how the oil patch worked to come see him. I figured I could hardly go wrong with a guy named Good. So I went to Enid, Oklahoma.

I spent a lot of time with Vaughn and his family. We went on the rigs. Studied geological data. Met with engineers. Kicked clods of dirt and squinted at the sun. We socialized too. Ate a lot of barbecue (not as good as Kentucky's). Drank beer. Learned the two-step. Went to *Tener's* in Oklahoma City and got some proper boots and a duster. I already had a cowboy hat.

Then came the moment of truth. Was I going to invest in the new wells Vaughn was fixin' to drill? I'd learned a lot about the oil business and I liked Vaughn a lot and respected his knowledge. He was a hands-on guy who'd been on the rigs and in the patch all his life. He didn't look a thing like J. R. Ewing and the other oil slicks on *Dallas,* but the proposed investment was sizable for me. And, unlike my other investments, I would have no control or influence over what happened once I put up my money. I was going back to Kentucky.. I hesitated.

> **LESSON FROM THE STREET #11**
>
> To deal with a negative, try raising it up front with a well-phrased question that anticipates the objection but is affirming at the same time.

Vaughn looked at me.

"Lacey, I know you're thinkin' this over pretty hard. I just want you to ask yourself one question. And I want you to know it doesn't matter to me how you answer it. Because either way you and I are going to be friends from now on. But the question you need to ask yourself is 'Can I afford to lose this money if the wells don't do what they should?'" He paused. "Because they may not."

I reached for my checkbook. Vaughn had asked the question that uncovered my fears. And he said it didn't matter to him what my decision was. Once my fear was up there flopping on the table where we both could see it, and Vaughn said it was fine with him either way, then my anxiety was assuaged. I put up the money. Vaughn may have been raised in the oil fields, educated without an Ivy League degree, but he sure didn't fall off the oil truck when it came to persuasion.

————

THE MOST POWERFUL QUESTION

One of the most powerful questions you can ask to uncover what people really care about is "That's an interesting price. Where did you get it?"

STREET-SMART REALITY
DON'T COUNTEROFFER; ASK A QUESTION

Steve Thompson was hired as president of a distilling company to be a change agent, to identify and develop new businesses. To that end, he put the distilling company in the fish farm business, which was quite a change indeed for this company that since 1870 had been mainly a maker and purveyor of distilled spirits.

After investing millions of dollars, including the purchase of hundreds of acres in Clarksdale, Mississippi, management became disillusioned with the time required to produce a profit at the fish farm.

"Sell it!" they told Steve.

In his initial efforts, Steve was able to turn up only one offer from an entrepreneur, Alvin, in Chicago, an offer several millions of dollars less than the distilling company had invested in the deal. I asked Steve where Alvin got his offering price.

"He didn't say."

"When are you going to meet again?"

"Two weeks in Chicago," he said.

"Well, after you have talked about the White Sox, the Cubs, the Bulls, and the Bears, ask him what he'll give you for the fish farm."

"He already told me."

"Ask him anyway. He may give you a higher figure. And if he gives you a lower one, you can remind him of your earlier conversation. "Once you settle on his offer, say to him: 'That's an interesting figure, Alvin. Where did you get it?'"

By asking Alvin where he got his number, Steve would help himself in a number of ways. First, Steve would not be challenging Alvin's number— a possible temptation—by saying something like, "That's ridiculously low. We have more than three times that much money in it."

Second, the question does not contain a counteroffer. Making a counteroffer without knowing the basis for the offer prematurely creates a bargaining zone within which any deal will be made, if one is to be made. The prices in this zone may not be in Steve's best interest even though he was the one who made the counteroffer.

Moreover, by merely asking where the number came from, Steve has the chance to learn what the potential buyer's thought process is as well as something about his hopes and fears about the deal. If, for example, Alvin has sharply depreciated the equipment in calculating the fish farm offer, there is a good chance he is concerned about having to replace it soon. This may or may not be a legitimate concern, but regardless of its legitimacy, it helps for Steve to be aware of what Alvin is thinking about the equipment and to deal with it if he can.

Convinced, Steve said he would call me on his return. He did and asked me to meet with him and his staff.

"Lacey, right after the small talk, I said, 'OK, this is like Bridge; let's review the bidding. What will you give us for the fish farm?'"

"Our bid is the same one I gave you on the phone."

"Then, I put the that's-an-interesting-price question to him and everything got really quiet. Alvin turned to his CFO and said, 'Where the hell did we get that price, David?'"

"Well, the CFO shuffled papers and then went to the flipchart and outlined the components of their price: So much for land, so much for improvements, so much for equipment, so much for fish."

"When he finished, I said, 'What about the fingerlings?'"

"What fingerlings?"

"There are thousands of fingerlings in these ponds," I told him.

"Yeah, but they don't have a market value," said the CFO.

"They will if you feed them."

After more back-and-forth, Alvin got his offer up by nearly another $1 million. Now, the deal didn't get done at that price; but the point is that Steve, by asking the powerful question, opened a dialogue that gave him information that led to a higher offer. Alvin's higher offer gave Steve a backup alternative during subsequent negotiations with an Indiana entrepreneur, who eventually bought the property.

> **LESSON FROM THE STREET #12**
>
> "That's an interesting price—where did you get it?" is one of the most powerful questions you can ask. Ask it; then listen.

The interesting-price question can take a number of forms: "That's an interesting delivery schedule. How did you arrive at it?" "That is an intriguing deal structure. What are your thoughts behind it?" "That is an interesting proposed rule (or regulation). What are the policy reasons on which it is based?"

————

Other Ways to Glean Information . . .
and Real Interests

You can also, of course, get valuable information from other sources to help you uncover the emotions and interests of those with whom you are bargaining.

THIRD-PARTY SOURCES OF INFORMATION

There are third party sources of information that reveal the real reasons behind what people say they want. You should try to uncover this information with due diligence. It can come from published reports about the business firms with whom you are dealing. It can come from the government. It can come from conversations with others.

Some of the information, though, may be unreliable. It may be hearsay. It may be outdated. It may be only partially correct. It may come from someone who has an axe to grind. Nevertheless, it is good to be aware of this information. Keep it in the back of your mind, and use it to develop hypotheses about both your partners and your opposers.

You can then test these hypotheses during the negotiation with information you obtain firsthand as you ask questions.

You can also gather nonverbal clues to what is going on in someone's heart and head by becoming a careful observer of body language.

BODY LANGUAGE

A lot has been written about body language. Some of what has been written is useful, and some is not. If a listener's arms are crossed, her mind is closed to your ideas. If she is scratching her head, she is weighing what you've said. If she rubs her eyes or sits with her finger pointing to her eyes, she cannot "see" your point. If, in answering your question she looks up and to the right, she is considering her answer. If she looks up and to the left, she is about to lie. Or is it the other way around?

That's the point. Body language can be a rough estimate of what is going on with the people on the other side of the table. If they have dozed off during your most persuasive arguments, you are probably not getting through to them. But too much weight can be given to nonverbal clues. The woman on the other side of the table, in folding her arms, may not be closed to your arguments; she may merely be trying to keep warm. Or, her chair may be without arms and this is a convenient way to rest without leaning on the table.

> **LESSON FROM THE STREET #13**
>
> Body language and third-party information can help uncover interests, but be skeptical of information gleaned only from these sources. Don't be afraid to rely on your gut feelings.

I consider nonverbal clues as only approximate indicators of what the other side may be feeling, but subtle nuances of what is going on are not easy to glean from body language.

Be aware of what you and the other folks are doing through gestures and facial expressions. Keep possible inferences in your mind. Test what you observe against all the facts and circumstances of what is happening. But be reluctant to draw a conclusion about the other side's hopes and fears merely from a raised eyebrow or a sidelong glance.

Know this: If you listen intently and watch closely, you will internalize a wide range of stimuli, and this internalization, though you may be unaware of it on a conscious level, will provide you with the intuition, or a gut feeling, about what is going on emotionally with the others at the table. This intuition will become part of your opinion about what is motivating the others to take the positions they do. When you test your hypotheses so formed by the statements made and answers given to the questions you ask, you'll begin to get a good idea of what is behind what is being said.

There are gaps between appearance and reality, between the reasons given and the real reasons. People don't necessarily try to deceive us—though they may—but they are often unaware of the difference between what they say and why they say it. It is our job to ferret out the hopes and fears behind what is said. Questions—powerful, tactful, probing questions—can help us do that. They can help us uncover emotions to reveal real interests. Then we have something to work with in our efforts to persuade.

DISCOVER EMOTIONS THAT BETRAY YOU

Fear, Confidence, and Anger

To manage is to foresee.

This was the mantra of Harvard Business School professor Georges F. Doriot. To manage anything better, he would say, you must try to see what is ahead—maybe not years ahead, but in the near term. What is around the corner? How will change affect the things that matter to you?

Foreseeing emotions is as important in managing as foreseeing events. Maybe more important.

Is your boss likely to say something to you today that will set you off? What possible fears and concerns will your co-workers have for not meeting their commitments? How will this affect you? What possible unexpressed anger is behind the work slowdown you've observed from your staff recently? What have you done or not done that may have caused this?

Being able to look ahead (and back) sets us apart from the other animals (that and our opposable thumb). A wolf doesn't visualize how he will get his next meal as we may visualize an upcoming job interview. He doesn't analyze why he missed that last rabbit as we may a lost sale. He just gets hungry and he hunts.

The wolf has emotions, of course. But he doesn't think about them, deal with them, reflect on their consequences. He reacts.

Thinking about emotions—ours and the people we try to persuade—understanding these emotions, foreseeing their likely occurrence, and acting to manage and direct these emotions can determine whether we *get it* in our life's negotiations.

Some highly respected authorities think that our emotions are like a cold. They just come over us and all we can do is treat the symptoms. Planning emotions, they think, is like trying to control a sneeze.

It is possible to anticipate and create conditions that are optimal for the emotions you wish to experience. It's not simple. You have to practice. But it's worth the effort.

It will help, first, to learn more about emotions.

Emotions from Your Caveman Ancestors . . . from Your Unique Experiences

I knew a pair of twins once whose parents had creatively named them Bob and Robert—like Dr. Seuss's Thing One and Thing Two. I called them Bob and Rob. Why their parents played this joke on the boys, I don't know; and I was too young to ask. But to understand emotions, there are some twins of the same name I must present to you: the Amy Gdala twins.

These are twin parts of your brain that govern some of your key emotions: together they are properly called the amygdalae.

These parts of your brain, and a few others such as the brain stem region, the hypothalamus, and the basal forebrain, induce most of your emotions. These small parts of the brain send commands to other parts of the brain and to the body. They send these commands through the bloodstream or along the neural system, the wiring network of our nerve endings. When these messages are sent, things begin to cook.

If your amygdalae are healthy and have not calcified (and this sometimes happens through disease), here is how the process works:

1. You see a snake. It has a triangular head and pits between its eyes.

2. You put this object in a class defined by your previous experience and knowledge, and the image activates all of the neural (nerve ending) sites that are prepared to respond to the representation of the particular class to which the snake belongs (i.e., things that slither along the ground). In this case, the sites that will be activated will be your two Amys—amygdalae—because they have been hardwired to respond. The hardwiring comes down from our cave-dwelling, slope-shouldered ancestors, but we modify the wiring based on our own experience with snakes. In other words, not everyone will react in the same way to seeing a poisonous snake. If you are a snake handler who can take up serpents and be not afraid, your reaction will be one thing. But if you spent several days in a Vietnamese field hospital recovering from a viper bite, your reaction will be something else again.

3. As a result of step 2, your amygdalae trigger signals to other brain sites and to your body. In this case, perhaps, fear and trembling and, in the extreme, physical illness may result from this communication. But again, the level of fear and its manifestations you experience and display will be a function of your hardwiring plus your own experience with this particular object.

In summary: An image is formed in our visual brain, a sector or sectors of the brain respond to the *type* of visual image formed, and all the chemical and nerve network responses come into play. Then, the experiences of your forebearer *pithecanthropus erectus* millions of years ago with an object like this, shaped by your own experience with snakes of this kind, produces a fear response.

This is the process for the formation of the major emotions—not just fear—that affect the things we want and whether we get them. With this in mind, we can begin to examine some specific emotions, and we can look at what effect their unchecked expression can have on our efforts to persuade others. Then, we can see what we can do about the results.

Fear and Paralysis . . .
Action and Mobilization

Not all fears, of course, produce negative results. Being afraid puts us on guard against the poisonous snake. We can then either avoid the snake by leaving the area at warp speed or kill it. Your reaction protects you. In his book *The Feeling of What Happens,*[1] professor Antonio Damasio demonstrates that if your amygdalae are calcified or otherwise impeded, you can get into all kinds of trouble. You aren't afraid of things you should be afraid of. You think everyone is your friend, and you act accordingly, often to your detriment.

Some fear or anxiety gives you an edge, keeps you on your toes, and prevents you from being overconfident, an emotion that in itself can lead you astray.

The experience of our own fears also makes it possible to recognize fear in others, and this can be very helpful.

A little fear, however, goes a long way. Fear can paralyze you or at least make your responses and reactions ineffective and slow. Remember the last time a possum crossed the road in front of your car at night, and the headlights seemed to freeze the animal? If the possum survived this meeting, your brakes—and not its survival instinct—probably saved the possum's life.

The same can happen to you if you are gripped by fear in a situation in which you have to give and take and respond to what is going on around you. You may be so possessed by the fear of a negative result that you can't think straight. So much may be at stake and the people on the other side so formidable that all your preparation seems for naught. You can't focus. Remember the struggles of Hamlet? To be or not to be? Should he kill himself? Fear gripped him. Should he kill his uncle? He feared that if he killed him while he was at prayer, his uncle would go to heaven. Fear made him waffle.

FEAR AND ITS PRICE—PARALYSIS

A manager of a small company that fabricated stainless steel for General Electric was required to negotiate a new agreement each year. Negotiating on behalf of GE was a purchasing veteran who each year negotiated contracts worth nearly $1 billion. Just prior to the expiration of the agreement each year this purchasing agent would write a letter to the company indicating that any agreement for the coming year would have to contain a "significant" price reduction. Sometimes the letter would even indicate a target reduction, like "10 percent off your current price to us." Since the GE business was half the dollar volume of the fabricator, and since GE could get the fabrication done elsewhere, the prospect of the annual negotiation created much anxiety at the smaller company.

The manager would prepare for the negotiation, but when the time came he would think of a reason not to go, and without a new contract the relationship between the companies would continue on a month-to-month basis at the original contract price.

> **LESSON FROM THE STREET #14**
>
> Action mobilizes you and overcomes the paralysis fear can produce.

After three years in this mode, the fabricator was being paid the same unit price it had received when the agreement commenced. The company began to lose money on GE. Necessity eventually outweighed the fear of taking a price reduction. The manager brought in a negotiation specialist, made him an officer of the company, and the company successfully concluded annual negotiations with GE thereafter, achieving price increases in each successive round of bargaining.

The manager finally stared his fear in the face and did something about it. But the paralysis created by the prospect of dealing with the 800-pound gorilla of GE and the prospect of an anticipated reduction cost the company money for three years.

When fear is *not* the dominant emotion motivating you in a negotiation, you are in a much better position to get what you desire from the interaction.

When you are unafraid, you are more open to the ideas of the other side, and this can have some very beneficial effects.

First, the other side may propose something as good or better for you than what you had thought was in your best interests. Don't laugh. It happens. If you enter a negotiation motivated by fear, you are predisposed to reject anything the other side proposes—or at least you won't consider it very seriously. In such a circumstance, motivated by fear, you are very likely to conclude that what is good for the other side could not possibly also be good for you. You look at everything in the negotiation as a "zero-sum game," any give-and-take transaction whose net result is zero. Whatever the other side gets, you gave up; and whatever you get, they gave up. You can see the zero-sum game attitude displayed nearly every day in the newspaper by each side in the Israeli/Palestinian disputes. Each side tends to view a gain by the other as their corresponding loss.

If, however, you are not afraid, you have a good chance to keep an open mind as both sides mutually explore solutions to the issues before you. You have a better chance, fearless, to seek joint gains for you and the other side.

Second, when you are unafraid, the other side can sense this. And they can likewise sense when you are fearful. They can do this because of the operation of their amygdalae. Your fear registers, or its absence does not, on your face, in your tone of voice, in your body language, in the things you say and the things you do not. Their senses communicate this to the amygdalae, which in turn communicate it to the rest of their brain. If the other side senses you are afraid of something, they may believe they have a decided edge in the negotiation. And they may have, if only because they believe they do.

The unafraid negotiator may be unafraid because of ignorance. Because of a lack of experience or because of the novelty of an undertaking, a negotiator may not know what she is up against. So, blissful in her pursuit, she accomplishes that which, had she known "better" she might have pursued more timidly, with less ardor, and therefore with less chance for success. She didn't know she couldn't do it. Or, as I would say about my dog Sport, "He doesn't know he's smaller than the big dogs."

In other words, sometimes too much knowledge is a hindrance to accomplishment. Too much information (about the size and resources of the people on the other side, the history of previous transactions, what is really at stake for you, and the like) can slow you down or paralyze you with fears and concerns.

STREET-SMART REALITY
KNOWLEDGE AND THE BENEFITS OF "IGNORANCE"

The purchasing agents of a giant motor manufacturing company frequently negotiate with suppliers who are partially owned by its own parent company in Japan. These suppliers know the motor manufacturing company has to buy from them as a sole source, although they are not truly the only sources for parts and materials used in making trucks and cars. This exclusive purchase requirement produces concern (fear) on the part of the agents for the manufacturing company, and it repeatedly affects their performance. Admonitions from a negotiation specialist to ignore this mandatory requirement of the negotiation proved unavailing.

A new hire, Toya, in the purchasing department was assigned a "sister company" negotiation, and the suggestion was followed that this agent be directed to negotiate with the supplier without the knowledge that the purchase from the supplier was mandatory. Toya knew only that the supplier had been reliable in the past, and for her to make a deal with them would be desirable.

> **LESSON FROM THE STREET #15**
>
> Someone without too much information can often provide a fresh look, a new insight, a different approach.

The agent prepared for the negotiation by obtaining a number of prices from other suppliers. She also got terms and delivery schedules. Her supervisor gave her the additional target challenge that she was to reduce the supplier's price of the previous year by 5 percent. During the negotiation, which was conducted in the presence but without the active involvement of her supervisor, the agents for the supplier coincidentally did not reveal their single-source status.

Through hard and creative bargaining, a part of which involved analyzing the supplier's cost structure and using the superior buying power of her company to lower the cost of certain parts to the supplier, Toya achieved a 2 percent reduction over the previous year's price. The supervisor was taken aback by her results.

When asked afterward what, if any, effect knowing of the sole source requirement may have had on her in the negotiation, Toya said simply, "It would have been like putting on my back a 100-pound sack of the parts I was buying!"

————

You can see that dealing with your own fears is tricky. Dealing with the fears of others can be even harder.

STREET-SMART REALITY
UNCOVERING THE FEARS OF OTHERS

Juan is a top executive with a major health insurance company. He is a veteran negotiator and routinely conducts negotiations with the largest hospitals in the country.

In a recent negotiation with one of these hospitals, Juan ran into an almost obsessive intransigence from Pam, the lead negotiator for the hospital. Nothing seemed to work. Juan suspected that she had latitude and authority to make concessions on some points, but she was like a tree standing by the water. She would not be moved on anything.

After several meetings with no progress, Juan decided to make some "collateral inquiries" by talking to other people he knew at the hospital to see if he could discover Pam's interests behind the hard-and-fast positions she was taking.

It took some time and the exercise of discretion, but he discovered that Pam believed that her job was at stake on this one negotiation. She feared if she didn't hit every one of her targets, she would be fired. Juan discovered a way, through an independent source, to assuage these fears—which were groundless anyway—and was able to reach agreements acceptable to both companies.

> **LESSON FROM THE STREET #16**
>
> People on the other side are concerned about something. What is it?

Juan was successful because he was able to deduce and then relieve or at least take the edge off Pam's fears of losing her job if she gave even an inch.

————

How do you deduce these fears on the other side? First, it should be clear by now that in every negotiation all of the participants are motivated by hopes and fears and, from time to time, by other emotions like anger and overconfidence. Your job is to discover what is behind the emotions on the other side. You can make some pretty good guesses, but sometimes you have to know with particularity.

At the threshold level, of course, the amygdalae will sense when the other side is fearful. Then, it is up to you, by building rapport and asking questions, to determine the exact nature of the fears and concerns in the current circumstance and to do something about them.

It is also helpful in dealing with fears to do something that the other side may not expect you to do. For example, there is a history of bad blood between your companies. If you find something in the past behavior of your company's representatives for which you can offer a genuine apology, then do it.

In making an apology against this history of animosity, you create what psychologists call "cognitive dissonance." Cognitive dissonance is a kind of anxiety created by simultaneously holding contradictory feelings. Here's how it works: You really like someone but strongly disapprove of his chain-smoking. You feel "conflicted." You feel anxiety about these contradictory feelings, and you tend to want to resolve that conflict. You can overcome the anxiety by deciding that you value this person so much you are going to overlook the bad habit. Or you can decide that the habit bothers you so much that you don't want to be around him. You act to eliminate the anxiety or conflict.

So, too, it is with your hypothetical apology. Your apology is unexpected, out of character for your company. This surprising behavior creates anxiety on the other side, which they wish to eliminate. Typically, the other side will resolve the conflict in your favor by, in this case, accepting your apology and softening their attitude toward you.

In a recent negotiation, the lead negotiator replaced a manager who had left the company. The departed employee, her replacement discovered during the negotiation, had misrepresented what the company would do in certain circumstances not specifically covered in the written contract. These misrepresentations were revealed during the negotiation, and the replacement negotiator dealt with the situation by apologizing professionally, if not profusely. She assured the other side that misrepresentation was not a company policy and that she would not tolerate it either in her staff or from anyone who asked her to mislead a business associate.

The apology was accepted. The table was reset between the parties. Bygones were bygones. The negotiation went forward and a deal was struck.

Underconfidence and Hesitation . . . Overconfidence and Imprudence

Fear and confidence have an inverse relationship. More fear, less confidence. Less fear, more confidence.

Fear affects confidence, but so do other factors. Some of these factors feed on each other. If you are unprepared, for example, you will feel less confident. You will also feel more fearful about any outcome because you lack confidence. You may also feel underconfident because of previous encounters with these same people. In a similar situation, you may not have done well in the past. This history affects your estimate of your present prospects, and, of course, may make you feel more fear about the coming negotiation. Or, you may lack confidence because you are generally pessimistic. Paradoxically, you may also lack confidence in a particular situation because you are fairly well informed, and you realize how much you do not know.

Whatever the reason for underconfidence, in my experience it is overconfidence that causes more mischief in negotiations. Overconfidence comes from many sources, sometimes simultaneously—and this makes it hard to deal with. It can come, for example, from too much reliance on "expert" opinion.

| STREET-SMART REALITY |
EXPERTS AND THE LULLING OF YOUR DISQUIETUDE

When I sold my house in Florida, I went to a local real estate guru who had a thriving real estate brokerage business. She gave me a figure. I thought it was high, but she was the expert. We put the house on the market at her number. In eighteen months that number did not attract one offer. Don't worry; we'll get our figure, she assured me. Still I stuck with it. Eventually, nearly two years later, I sold the house for about 40 percent less than her estimate of its value and, by the way, through a different broker but with no hard feelings between me and the guru.

The lesson? I was overly biased by "expertise" and by the anchor price she came up with. The price took on a life of its own, and the longer I stuck with it, the more I believed it, until finally I didn't believe it anymore.

> **LESSON FROM THE STREET #17**
>
> Listen to experts, but don't let them lull your disquietude. No one cares as much about your interests as you do.

———

Overconfidence can arise also, one may argue, "naturally." That is, we *Homo sapiens* are naturally egocentric. We tend to look at everything from our own perspective, and we don't give sufficient weight to how the other side sees things. We give a lot of thought to how we think the other side should see things but not very much to how they very likely *do* see them.

If you attend one of our negotiation seminars, you'll have a chance to win a crisp $20 bill. We auction it off to the highest bidder in increments of at least $1 per bid. I first saw this auction at Northwestern University's Kellogg School, but we have conducted it ourselves hundreds of times in the past ten years. The unique aspect of this auction is that the second-highest bidder also has to pay us his bid but he does not get the $20 bill.

As you reflect on these conditions of the auction, you may think you would sit out this exercise and not bid. Yet, in the classroom the pattern is roughly the same every time we do it. At first, there are a number of bids from around the room, but soon the bidding comes down to two people. At about the level of $14 and $15 bids, it becomes clear what is going on. If the second-highest bidder does not top the highest, he will have a sure loss of his current bid. If he goes $1 higher, then he may win if the other bidder drops out. But when he goes up $1, then the previous high bidder is in exactly the same situation that he was in the last round. And so it goes.

Only when the bidders begin to look at things from the perspective of the other bidders, do they realize what their self-centered perspective has got them into. Amazingly, once, in a room full of executives with strong egos, slapping checkbooks and gold cards on the table, the bidding passed $5,000—for a $20 bill!

You're curious: Did we take the money? No. We let them off with a warning for permitting their emotions to overload their judgment and gave each final bidder a prize in recognition of their fearless, if egomaniacal, bidding.

This auction contains many lessons about negotiation, but one of the most notable is the way overconfidence can lead us astray as we negotiate.

Another way overconfidence leads us astray is related to the lesson of the auction. It is a phenomenon I call "I-am-smart-enough-for-both-of-us." In the first chapter of this book I told of an experience with a Florida church. The deal the church could not refuse is a good example of the "I-am-smart-enough-for-both-of-us" trap. I thought I knew what was best for me and for the church. This led me to be very firm and inflexible in my position, and by the time I realized this, I almost ran out of time with my lender.

When you believe that you are right—that you know what is best for each side—you are led to extreme positional bargaining. If you are right, why should you give in on an issue just because the other side is too dumb to know what is best for them?

Part of the explanation of why we hold a position long after it has become untenable is that in addition to being right, we wrongly believe that being tough is the best way to get what we want. The "nuke-'em-till-they-glow" negotiators have reputations as the best negotiators. So we're not ourselves going to be pushovers. We're going to be immovable.

But in my experience a stubborn refusal to budge results in an impasse and no deal much more often than it produces what the "tough" negotiator wants.

The expertise we have spoken of in any field, but particularly in medicine and law, contributes to the "I am right" errors in negotiation. Most of the time, however, the expert has no more monopoly on insight than the inexperienced person on the other side of the table. When you have information the other side doesn't have, and this information gives you status as an "expert," how you present this "advantage" becomes very important to the outcome of your attempts to persuade.

STREET-SMART REALITY

OVERCONFIDENCE AND ITS CARICATURE, ARROGANCE

A fast-food giant wanted to reacquire some of its franchise stores. The company put together a hotshot acquisition team of recent MBA graduates, some of whom had Wall Street investment banking experience. They "did" the numbers on reacquisitions and came up with a fairly narrow range of prices to offer. They were negotiating with store owners around the country who were savvy businesspeople in running their restaurants but had little or no experience in buying and selling restaurants.

> **LESSON FROM THE STREET #18**
>
> Don't be extravagant with displays of what you know. That almost never helps you get what you want.

In most of the negotiations, the company acquisition team held fast to its expertly derived numbers. And, in most cases, the negotiations produced no-deal results. Only when the team regrouped and reflected on the feedback they received from the "nonexpert" sellers did they move off their original prices and begin to make some deals.

A great American once said, "I'd rather be right than be president." This surprising, no-compromise statement came from one of the great compromisers of all time, Henry Clay. But perhaps his claim was prophetic. Serving in the United States Senate, he was right about a number of monumental issues facing the United States of his day. But he was never president.

Too often, after much preparation and analysis, businesspeople, brimming with overconfidence, become so convinced they are right that they miss opportunities to make deals that would be good, if not perfect, for them. Compromise. It's a good concept with a bad reputation. You must give if you expect to get. They call it reciprocity. A bawdy character in the musical *Chicago* defines reciprocity and hits the concept dead on: "If you're good to Mama, Mama's gonna be good to you."[2]

Anger—in You, a Big Disadvantage for Yourself . . . in Others, a Possible Advantage for You

Someone once said that if you speak in anger you'll give the best speech you'll ever live to regret.

Why would that necessarily be true? Because such a speech contains barbs pointed at someone who provoked (or you believe provoked) your anger. Hurling these barbs, inspired by your anger, makes you feel better. You hurt those who hurt you. These barbs, however, when they find their mark, often produce even more pointed responses, which in turn produce more retaliation. In the end, much mischief and considerable damage is done by speaking in anger. Collaboration in negotiation is frustrated by these angry words that are hard to retract, and in the end people on all sides of an issue may become demoralized by the anger of one or more of the participants.

Rage, fury, wrath, hatred, indignation (brought on by anger), irritation— anger is a hydra-headed monster we each live with. I say we live with it because anger is so closely connected to our psyche as to be almost indistinguishable from it. It is part of who we are and how we see ourselves. And, in fact, in my experience almost all anger arises, in its various forms, because of a real or perceived blow to the way we see ourselves or the way we think others see us—in other words, from a blow to our egos.

These blows are powerful. They hit us where we live. They strike at who we think we are.

Examples of the effects of anger are abundant in family life. The most gut-wrenching example of anger on that front arises from the real or suspected infidelity of a spouse. In our culture, we regard fidelity as a right or at least as a privilege, and when a real or an imagined provocation leads us to believe this right or privilege has been violated, anger, often even murderous anger, is the result. Shakespeare's Othello murders his beloved Desdemona because he has been led to believe, wrongly it turns out, that she has been unfaithful. Even his great love for her was overpowered by his anger. Belatedly discovering his mistake, Othello kills himself, asking that he be remembered as one who loved "not wisely but too well."[3]

This last statement contains an incongruity that is instructive on the issue of anger and how it can stymie your efforts to persuade others. How can it be that you could love so "well" that you kill not only the object of your affection but yourself as well?

Maybe, you say, people back in Elizabethan times, the time of Shakespeare, were just more dramatic than we moderns. It would make some sense, after all, for the leading dramatist of all time to live during a period of high drama. But these powerful passions of "love" persist today and find expression in our contemporary culture.

Ego-connected anger is a major reason parties to even a rather simple divorce can almost never represent themselves. They need lawyers to keep them apart. Now, it is unfortunately true that lawyers and other third parties in divorces can foment more conflict than otherwise may be present. Nevertheless, left alone, parties to a split-up can hardly be expected to bring their once-close relationship to a harmonious end by themselves—even putting aside their need for assistance on purely legal issues.

They care too much about what is going on. There is too much ego involvement. The kids—extensions of themselves—are something to be angry about and battle over. The "sticks"—the furniture and other property—much of it acquired together and with much ego investment—is often another point of angry contention.

It's hard to quarrel with Shakespeare's choice of words—a man you have to agree had a way with words—but having Othello say that he loved not wisely but too well may have misnamed what Othello felt for Desdemona. Again, it's hard to square loving someone so "well" that you kill them.

Perhaps what he meant is not loving so well but so intensely, so strongly, in such a way that your ego is so tied up with the object of your affection that a real or perceived provocation is a personal blow and can produce a powerfully self-destructive retaliation.

> **LESSON FROM THE STREET #19**
>
> Anger is something to expect in ourselves and in others, so get ready for it.

Remember the hospital negotiator who believed that her job hinged on the one negotiation with Juan, the insurance company executive? Pam saw every issue on the table as an issue personal to her, to her career, to her immediate economic survival. She cared, not wisely but, as Shakespeare would have it, too well, too intensely. She saw herself personally so bound up in every issue that she could not negotiate wisely.

So, in matters that we care about, that our egos are bound up in, we run the real risk of becoming angry, especially as we encounter people who disagree with how these matters or issues should be dealt with and resolved.

Think about these scenarios:

- Your supervisor gives you a 4 out of a possible 5 in the category "takes initiative" during an evaluation period when you were solely responsible for beginning three new projects, two of which are already profitable. You didn't get a 5, and you get angry.

- You are part of a three-person negotiation team. The chief negotiator on the other side pointedly ignores your comments and offerings, and you are the most experienced person at the table. You get angry.

- I offered the Florida church a deal too good for them to refuse. They refused it. I got angry.

Euripides said that those whom God wishes to destroy he first makes mad. There is some question over whether by "mad" he meant "angry" or "crazy." Maybe it doesn't matter, because anger makes us crazy and produces self-destructive results.

What matters is that we understand anger in ourselves and others, recognize it, prepare for it, and manage it.

A SHOW OF ANGER AS A TACTIC

It is true, of course, that sometimes anger or the appearance of it can be used as a tactic. In the famous "kitchen debate" between Russian premier Khrushchev and vice president Richard Nixon at the Moscow Exhibition in 1959, there was much finger pointing, lapel tugging, and face reddening as the two men debated the comparative merits of their two systems of government. Each tried to seem more pugnacious than the other. But careful observers, like Harrison Salisbury of the *New York Times,* characterized the angry exchange as a "show" put on by both men.

A show of anger is usually not a good idea as a tactic. It is too easy for the act to become real; and even if it does not, your playacting, if discovered, will badly damage your credibility. But it is important to consider that the anger being displayed on the other side may not be genuine. The harsh words, the personal attack, may be an act. If that is your conclusion, you may choose to ignore the act. Or, you may pretend that the anger is real and deal with it as if it were, which we shall discuss shortly.

REAL ANGER AS DESTRUCTIVE

Real anger can be fatal to the constructive discussion and resolution of issues in personal lives, in the political arena, and in business.

My friend Opal Lee, the coal mogul, who made and then broke what would have been a very profitable deal for her, was motivated by a form of anger: indignation. She was indignant that I was going to make money for being *merely* a broker. She thought I was getting something for very little or nothing. She got indignant, and we had no deal. Now, maybe my deal wouldn't have kept Opal Lee from going broke, but it might have helped.

I also learned a good deal about the effects of real anger in the dry-cleaning business.

STREET-SMART REALITY
ANGER AND WHAT TO DO WITH IT

At one point I had a thriving and profitable dry-cleaning business in Kentucky and three thriving and unprofitable such businesses in Florida. It took a lot of hands-on management to get the profits from the one to offset the losses from the other three, so I was in the Florida stores a lot.

Most people who use dry cleaners are very particular about their clothes. They wear their emotions about their attire on their sleeves, so to speak.

If you crush their buttons and don't replace them or replace them with buttons of a different size; if you don't get out the stain that has permanently dyed the fabric of their dress; if an article of their clothing goes temporarily (you hope) missing; if a stain becomes, while in your care, a hole—if any of these or myriad other missteps occur, it is a big deal, a deal big enough to provoke anger.

And when customers complain about what has happened, it is never when you are there alone so the issue can be handled discreetly. It's always when the store is full of customers.

I remember Mr. Bresson, who taught me something about anger in myself and in others during my dry-cleaning days.

He burst through the double glass doors at the Dixie Highway location like John Wayne coming into a bar to get the bad guys. He was waving an oversized silk handkerchief. The store was full of people, and I was the only counter help.

"You have put a hole in my pochette!" he barked.

His charming French accent wasn't so charming, I noticed, as I was introduced to a pochette, or pocket square, with a hole in it.

"Look, look. I brought this in to you with a stain and you have given it back to me with a hole. This is a Hermes pochette and it cost $100. My wife gave it to me for our anniversary!"

My first reaction was to respond with the same vigor of his complaint.

"Monsieur Bresson, we could not have put a hole in your pochette. Our chemicals are so mild you can soak your hands in them. Our equipment is state of the art. Our people are trained in the care of delicate fabrics."

"Hermes doesn't make a delicate pochette. Hermes is a French manufacturer, not American. You could pull an automobile with that pochette!"

This last was at a decibel level higher than his first sally.

"We used generally accepted dry-cleaning practices to clean that pochette, Monsieur Bresson. Perhaps there has been a failure in the weaving, something went wrong in the warp and the weft in the silk." Showing a little expertise would put him off balance, I thought, but I thought wrong.

"I don't care about 'generally accepted' or 'warp and weft.' I just know you put a hole in my pochette. So what are you going to do about it? And by the by, stop calling me 'Monsieur.' This is America."

My Francophile effort to build rapport having failed, I tried a different approach. "Why don't I send your pochette to the International Fabricare Institute. We are a member," I said proudly. "Let's see what they say."

"I don't care what they say! I only care what you say! So what do you say?"

As I considered my response, he went on.

"And another thing. My wife picked up a black cocktail dress from you last week. And it was so wrinkled that we had to take it to One Hour Martinizing—at our inconvenience and cost I may add—to get it re-pressed so she could wear it that evening."

Now, things were escalating. A hole in a pochette—something that arguably could happen because of manufacturing defects, age of the garment, the owner's negligence, a number of factors outside our control—had grown to a complaint about pressing. Pressing is something for which a dry cleaner cannot easily deflect responsibility. And then there was the unfavorable comparison to a competitor.

Meanwhile, the other customers were enjoying the show. What was Lacey going to do? How would this drama end? What implications did it have for their own clothes in my care?

Before I say what happened with Mr. Bresson, let me pass along to you the lessons I learned about anger from this experience.

First of all, it was a mistake for me to be defensive about the very real possibility that we had put a hole in the silk. Mr. Bresson, after all, didn't care about my chemicals, or my equipment, or how well I trained my people. Mentioning all of this just made him assert his complaint more loudly and insistently. He wanted the hole fixed.

When I offered a solution (the International Fabricare Institute),which he understandably saw as a put-off, he got angrier.

We were both angry—he at what he saw as a cleaning misdeed, exacerbated by my tap dancing around the problem, and me at his calling into question my competence and honesty in front of other customers.

Wasn't this, you may say, much ado about very little? Maybe. But consider this: Mr. Bresson, like many of us, showed a close affinity with his clothes. His clothes reflected how he saw himself and how he perceived others saw him. My dry-cleaning business, at one time the premier dry cleaner for the area, was a reflection of how I saw myself and how I perceived others saw me. The hole in the pochette and our reactions to it delivered blows to our egos, our perceptions of ourselves and others' views of us. Anger swept over us and threatened a good business relationship.

> **LESSON FROM THE STREET #20**
>
> When someone is angry, let them get it out. Then say, "Well . . ."; then, let them get the rest out. Don't debate. Deflate.

After Mr. Bresson, and other similar experiences, I prepared to forfend against them. I adopted what I came to call my best "undertaker posture" when confronted by angry customers.

Undertakers have a sensitive job. In their line of work, emotions are always high. Tears are just a word away. Their choice of the wrong word can hurt someone and hurt their business. Most of the time, they don't say much. They stand with their hands clasped in front of them, look concerned, and make generally supportive but usually indecipherable sounds.

"Mmmm. Uh, huh . . . Oh, yes . . . mmmmmm."

They don't give you much to react to. I decided that is what I would do with the Mr. Bressons of my world. The solution was three easy steps:

1. I would listen intently to their complaints. I would say little or nothing until I was fairly certain they had run out of steam. Then I would stick my toe in the water.

2. "Well. . . ." Then I would pause. Sometimes just a word from me would get them going again. But after I was fairly certain they had run down, I would do this: I would reach for a notebook and pen, and I would say,

3. "Now, Mr. So and So, let me see if I understand what you are saying. You call this a 'pochette.' How do you spell that? And where did you get it? And how long have you had it? And how much did it cost?"

This approach had several benefits. In the first place, it let the customer vent and run out of steam. Then, by writing down the complaint I demonstrated at least two things: I cared about the problem, and having made a record, presumably, I was going to do something about it.

Plus, by putting the issue on paper, I objectified the problem between us, so we became side-by-side problem solvers, even pointing to what I had written, instead of human dragons breathing hotter and hotter fire on each other.

This is not to say that every such encounter and negotiation ended happily for each party. But most of the time it did.

Monsieur Bresson? The pochette was about two years old, so he agreed to a 50 percent discount off the original price. Since he was a good customer, I offered and he accepted $50 worth of free dry cleaning over the following two months. It cost me about $10 for his continued goodwill.

———

ANGER IN DISGUISE

It is helpful, if not pleasant, to know someone is angry and to know why as you try to persuade the person of something you want. If you are unaware of people's feelings, if you misperceive their state of mind, you may say or do things that will be counterproductive to your objectives. How can you be unaware of someone's anger? Maybe you're obtuse. But more than likely you are unaware because people often disguise their feelings, because hiding their feelings is tactically the wise thing to do. Or because expressing anger at what has provoked their feelings can make them look bad, small, petty.

STREET-SMART REALITY
WHOSE ANGER?

Lucretia felt her supervisor had been attacking her for several days. Rick would go out of his way to embarrass her about the new marketing initiative their department had undertaken. He found myriad small things about which to criticize her. She was puzzled. Finally, in frustration and at no small risk, she made a point of running into Rick's boss and bringing up what she had been experiencing. Jonas was likewise puzzled, but said he'd get back to her. A few days later he called.

"Lucretia, don't worry. Rick's not upset with you. He's mad at me for all the travel this new program has put on him and he's taking it out on you."

Hey, that's not fair, you may think, especially if you're Lucretia. But Rick's is a common response in organizations of all kinds. Someone on a rung above you does something that angers you and, unable to seek redress against the more powerful, you direct your response against someone with less power—your subordinate on a lower rung.

Rick's boss may not, without the "accidental" communication with Lucretia, have known about Rick's anger at him, and the difficulty this anger created in the department could have spread unaccountably.

Lucretia, for example, may have directed her anger response to Rick's attacks toward a co-worker or a subordinate, threatening, with this successive round of actions, the marketing initiative of the department and perhaps even the careers of the individuals involved.

ANGER JU JITSU

People sometimes don't take their anger out on scapegoats like Lucretia but rather on the actual provocateur, but they do it in an indirect manner. They become, in a clinical phrase that has become popular, "passive-aggressive."

Your partner criticizes you for running the dishwasher when it is only half full. You respond, not defensively or with an angry riposte, but by filling the washer so full that it is nearly impossible to open the door, and some of the dishes don't get clean. You want a full dishwasher? Okay, I'll show you full!

You insist on being paid by the tenth of the month, and that is highly inconvenient for my company. All right, I'll send you a check arriving on the tenth but drawn on an account in the Bahamas that will take ten days to clear.

ANGER IN CODE

Spoken words may have a common understanding among most people, but when they are used in a particular context, they are barbs aimed at the listener. The words may be a code.

After David Maraniss, a reporter with the *Washington Post,* had written a critical biography of then-president Bill Clinton, a book Maraniss characterizes as "honest," he didn't look forward to his first encounter with the president after the book's publication.

He was more than mildly taken aback when at a public forum where Maraniss was being recognized, Clinton greeted him with a big grin, appraised him up and down and said, "Hi, David. Congratulations on your award. Nice tie."

Puzzled, Maraniss sought an explanation from longtime Clinton aide George Stephanopolous.

In that context, Stephanopolous said, "nice tie" meant "David, f___ you!"[4]

Now, Clinton may have been practicing cognitive dissonance. Or maybe in such a situation he was trying to control his actual feelings by finding something positive to say to someone to whom he would like to say something negative. Maybe it doesn't matter. What does matter to you, though, is that you figure out whether the words spoken to you are friendly words or angry words dressed up as friends.

You may think—"Whoa! I don't want to be so sensitive that I can detect every negative nuance directed at me. I'll be chronically depressed."

Perhaps, but wouldn't you rather know the reality behind what folks say to you?

Some people would rather not know. Other people, however, simply cannot know. See if you are one of those.

ANGER AND THE IRREPRESSIBLE

Hubert Humphrey, then a Minnesota senator, was visiting a factory while campaigning for president in 1960. As he approached workers on the assembly lines, he would speak to them, and one of his aides would record the workers' responses. One worker engaged Humphrey in an exchange that would have unnerved most candidates.

"Hey, Mr. Humphrey, when you were mayor in Minneapolis I heard that you tried to raise taxes seven times. And I heard that you founded the ADA (Americans for Democratic Action) and that this became a Communist-front organization. And, by the way, you've said some real anti-Catholic statements about Jack Kennedy. Shame on you!"

> **LESSON FROM THE STREET #21**
>
> Be an anger detective. Find out who is mad at whom.

After some efforts to deflect these criticisms, Humphrey and his entourage moved on to the next worker.

As they walked to the next station on the line, Humphrey turned to his aide who was writing furiously on his clipboard.

"Better put that guy in the undecided column," Humphrey said.[5]

Perhaps it was this irrepressible optimism that made Humphrey believe, eight years later when he was vice president, that he could win the presidency without disassociating himself completely from the increasingly unpopular Vietnam war that his boss, Lyndon Johnson, drew us more deeply into with each passing year of his presidency.

Alternatively, perhaps this unfailingly positive (in spite of the facts) outlook got Humphrey through some very tough times in his political as well as his personal life.

A famous trial attorney once told me about one of his clients.

"What John doesn't realize is that, while I make little effort to disguise it, I can't stand him. But he keeps treating me like his best friend. It's a little unnerving."

In figuring out the real feelings of those with whom you are dealing, I come down on the side of reality—even if I don't come out too well in the eyes of others. It's better to know. And in assessing whether you have given offense to someone or for some unaccountable reason they have taken offense at something you have said or done, don't kid yourself.

Remember: anger takes many forms, for example, indignation and hurt feelings. You need to identify anger, and other emotions that can derail your efforts to get what you want, understand them, and bring them into your control for your own benefit.

PART TWO

HOW YOU SHOULD PREPARE TO GET IT!

4

PREPARE TO GET IT!

The What, Who, Where, and When of Persuasion

You are now aware of how important emotions are to your success in persuading others. But being aware is not enough. You've got to prepare. A useful way to remember how to prepare to persuade is summarized in a little ditty from Rudyard Kipling:

> I keep six honest serving men
> (They taught me all I knew);
> Their names are What and Why and When
> And How and Where and Who.[1]

In preparation, in other words, just remember to ask yourself, *what, who, where,* and *when*—and *why* and *how?*

What Do *You* Want . . . *What* Do *They* Want?

To begin your preparation, ask yourself: *What* do both parties want? What do *you* want? This is a threshold consideration. If you are uncertain about what you want, you'll have a hard time getting it. The "it" will elude you because it's hard to hit a fuzzy or moving target. Test yourself: Can you express what you want in thirty (or fewer) seconds? No? Then what you want is not clear to you.

Next, examine what *they* want. How do they express this? In words? Body language? By what they do? By what they have done in the past? This is all part of taking inventory of each side's positions and their interests. What do they say they want, and what are the emotions driving them to take these positions?

WHAT DO YOU WANT?

What are the goals on your side? These goals should be expressed as narrowly as possible. What are the times of delivery you seek, the prices, the specifications, the contingencies, the place of performance? What is your Range of Acceptable Settlement (your "RAS")? In other words, what is a reasonable top and bottom for your side? And how did you reach these figures or terms? You must be prepared to explain and, moreover, rigorously demonstrate where you got these figures or terms and why they are reliable, rooted in reason, and not just mythical constructs based on your wildest dreams. After all, the people on the other side may read this book. They may say to you, "That's an interesting figure; where did you get it?" You should be prepared to answer fully even if you choose not to answer at all.

> **LESSON FROM THE STREET #22**
>
> If you prepare better than the other side does, you'll do better nine times out of ten.

In evaluating your RAS, note that if you are ambitious about your goals, you are likely to be more successful. But it is easy, if you are not careful, to cross the line of asking too much or offering too little and thereby to risk a no-deal result.

LOWBALLING AND HIGHBALLING

Some say that if you are a buyer you should "lowball" the seller—offer a ridiculously low figure because "you can always come up." But can you always recover from an extreme position, save face (yours and the other side's), and make a deal out of a different and reasonable figure? Not always. Sometimes a lowball price will drive potential sellers away from the table permanently with some bad feelings in the process. You have insulted them. Or, even if they are not insulted, they may conclude that you and they are so far apart that further discussion is useless.

STREET-SMART REALITY
LOWBALLING

There was a hotel of fading elegance in Palm Beach, Florida, that I was interested in buying. It had no parking. I suspected it might have mildew in the walls. I saw a lot of mold. Its structural integrity was suspect. And it was small, about fifty rooms. But it was in a city where a small jewel of a hotel would be in great demand. I arranged to meet with the owners, a husband and wife, in the hotel where they lived.

They were a fascinating couple. They had been in Hungary when the Russian tanks rolled in and took over. They had suffered much loss and deprivation. In America they had flourished, especially by old-country standards. They were justifiably proud of their accomplishments. And I listened to their story with great interest and admiration. We spoke together for hours and drank strong Hungarian coffee; and when I thanked them and left, I believed they really wanted to sell their property to me. We had built considerable rapport. They were asking around $4 million, which I considered high. I didn't tell them that though. Nor did I ask them where they got the $4 million figure. From our conversation, I inferred it was based on the sweat and tears and the love their efforts to own and run the place had engendered. They didn't have any spreadsheets.

I met my real estate agent at TooJay's, a nearby restaurant, and we hammered out an offer. The best I could do was around $2 million, given the uncertainty and the fact that I would have to acquire off-site parking at an indeterminate, but probably high, price, or I would have to shuttle people to and from space I could lease in an existing parking lot, also at a high price. There was the issue, too, of the small number of possible rooms that would result in the conversion.

I made the decision that my agent would tender the offer to the couple without me while I waited at the restaurant. In a while he returned. His usually deeply tanned face wasn't so brown. He looked washed out.

"They are furious with you," he said. "You've insulted them, and they don't want me to bring you around there again. I'm not sure they would even see me if I brought them another potential buyer."

It was not, of course, my intention to insult the couple whom I considered my new friends. I had armed my agent with all of the reasons for my offer, which he presented to them; but their reaction, after I had thought about it in the succeeding days, was instructive to me.

In the first place, I should have gone with the offer myself. This deals in part with the *who* part of the Kipling quote, and I'll return to consider this later. Further, the experience taught me the danger of lowballing. I was not, of course, pegging my price as a tactic to get the couple to adjust their unrealistic expectation of a $4 million sale. But, the effect was the same as if I had been. No deal. And no possibility of resetting the table to make a deal.

> **LESSON FROM THE STREET #23**
>
> Don't lowball, thinking you can always go up later. There may not be a later.

If you are a buyer, don't think you can go in rock bottom low and then raise the ante later. There may not be a later.

The rest of the story: The hotel was sold twice after my unsuccessful offer. The first buyer paid about what I had offered, couldn't make the arithmetic work, and took a big loss. My mistakes taught me a lesson, and, by accident, I missed a financial disaster.

———

You can create great bargaining power and credibility by making your first offer a fair one, but one that works for you. Sometimes, if you are more than fair, good things will happen for you. I learned this from a former business partner.

STREET-SMART REALITY
HIGHBALLING

In my early years in the coal business, Jim Smith, who was my partner in some of these coal enterprises, and I traveled around leasing coal from the farmers under whose farms the coal lay. In our efforts we competed with some of the giant coal companies of the day: Peabody, P&M, Consolidated. These companies had something of an edge going in because they were huge and on that basis alone may have been considered more likely actually to mine the coal and therefore produce royalties for the farmers. Jim shocked me, at first, by offering royalties that were well into the upper quartile of what would be considered our RAS. He would always make his offer this way: "Folks, I don't have much time here today, but I have studied your coal reserves; and I think a fair price would be $X per ton."

Usually there was very little dickering. More often than not the farmer would say something like "Well Jim, if you think that is fair, why, we'll just go right along with you."

After watching this process for a while, and being aware that Peabody and others were offering lower royalties than we were and getting some takers, I suggested to Jim that we were leaving money on the table, and he said something that stuck with me. "The price we're offering will spread all around the coalfields. And when we sit with these farmers, they'll have confidence in what we say and will want to make a deal with us. They'll know we're not trying to skin 'em."

> **LESSON FROM THE STREET #24**
>
> Make a fair offer and
> your credibility goes up.

It worked, and we got some good leases we may not otherwise have had a chance to get. Lowballing was not a part of Jim's working vocabulary. What Jim did may be called highballing, and, although I have rarely seen it done, it gave us great negotiating power.

If you are a seller, take a hard look at what you consider to be your Range of Acceptable Settlement, and set an asking price that is defensible, but high enough to put the other side on notice that your expectations are ambitious. Psychologically, a high ask may cause the buyers to reevaluate an unrealistically low offer they were considering.

As the seller, you should be prepared to make the first offer. After all, if that is your product, you ought to know how much you want for it

- How much will it cost to make a few hundred widgets?

- If you are a consultant, how much do you charge for a two-day seminar?

- How much will you take for a small division that no longer fits your company's line of business?

If you are the seller and you make an I-will-take offer, the price, whatever it is, has the powerful effect of anchoring the negotiation. This price is the starting point and all else flows from it. If you doubt this, consider how powerful is the anchoring effect of the prices in the multiple real estate listings. This anchoring does not occur because the prices are somehow rigorously market derived and then enshrined in the listings. Most often these prices are the result of conversations between owners and realtors and may bear only accidental relationship to the actual value of the houses. The owners often overvalue their houses, and the realtors, eager to obtain a listing, tend to agree with an owner's valuation—at least until they get the listing contract. Nevertheless, these are the prices from which the bargaining begins. Frequently, if a buyer is interested, his offer will be in response to the listing price, and the two prices will form a zone of possible agreement, within which a deal, if one is to be made, will be struck.

In preparation, there are first-move advantages and disadvantages in the persuasion polka; but you should be prepared to go first, especially if the other side is not forthcoming. After all, you don't want to end up like those playboy Frenchmen, Alphonse and Gaston, who were so deferential in wishing the other to pass first through the door at which they had simultaneously arrived ("After you, Alphonse." "No, after you, Gaston.") that they both missed the party.

Remember, too, if the other side shoots you a price, term, or condition, don't immediately validate the offer by making a counter. Instead, say, "That's an interesting price; where did you get it?"

WHAT DO THEY WANT?

Your preparation will be incomplete if you do not make a careful estimate as well of what the other parties to the negotiation want.

- What do those on the other side say they want?

- What do they say they will or will not do?

- What ambitions and hopes, concerns and fears seem to be driving them?

To answer these questions requires some effort. It involves understanding the other side's business, its markets, its corporate or organizational goals, and the forces affecting its actions.

Remember the Japanese automaker required to do business with sister companies and the "reverse engineering" they did to reach their price reduction goals? This involved a truly thorough understanding of the other companies—their cost structure, who their suppliers were, what leverage the bigger company could bring to bear on these suppliers, and the like.

In further understanding the other side's position, pay careful attention not only to the fat documents of many pages that are trotted out as offers or responses, but also to what those on the other side say both before and during the negotiations.

A key is to look for consistencies and contradictions not only in what is said, but also between what is said and what others do and have done in the past. Most likely, this is not your first negotiation with these people, and what has happened with them in the past has a good chance of being repeated in the present deal. What is past is prologue.

Keep in mind, too, that what the other side says it wants may reveal only its *position* on a particular issue. What others say may not reveal *why* they take this position.

An environmental organization wants a bridge built downtown, but not east of town. That's the group's position. The why of this position may be that most of the organization's members live on exclusive east-end estates, and they believe an east-end bridge will disturb their lifestyles and drive their property values into the ground. A downtown merchants' organization, on the other hand, may prefer an east-end location for such a bridge, and this position has its whys as well. We'll talk about the why of preparation in the next chapter.

ISSUES/POSITIONS/INTERESTS—PREPARATION ON STEROIDS

In my experience, every negotiation, like all of Gaul (in that famous quote we learned in high school Latin), may be divided into three parts.

- First, there is the issue or issues involved: Should we, for example, build another bridge? Or two?

- Second, there are the positions of the parties: No. Yes, one downtown. Yes, one in the east end. Yes, two bridges.

- Third, there are the interests of the parties: We cannot afford a bridge. A downtown bridge will protect east-end property values. An east-end bridge will be better for downtown merchants. Two bridges will address all traffic and economic development issues.

This is a useful framework when you have little time to prepare.

LESSON FROM THE STREET #25

When time to prepare is tight, remember: Issues, Positions, Interests.

Your boss summons you to his office to present your recommendations on an issue involving your company and a major supplier. You have ten minutes to prepare. Don't panic. Just ask yourself: What are the major *issues* between my company and the supplier? What are the *positions* the parties have taken on these issues? What are the *interests* underlying these positions? What, in other words, are the hopes and fears (or ambitions and concerns) of my boss with respect to our positions? What are the hopes and fears driving the supplier on its positions? Do I personally have any dogs in this fight? What, for example, is at stake for me personally in this controversy? Are my interests the same as those of my boss? When you have asked and answered these questions, go to your boss's office. You are passably, if not thoroughly, prepared to make your recommendation.

I have found that this "issues/positions/interests—preparation on steroids," as I call it—is good when time is tight. And don't forget to take into account your own personal interests. They may be different from those of your company.

A good way to keep track of this preparation short-cut approach is to create a Target Inventory sheet. Replicate the one here for your own use, and fill it out each time there is a time crunch and you cannot undertake a full-scale preparation. Fill out one sheet for each issue in the negotiation.

You have addressed the *what* of your interaction. Now take a look at the *who*.

TARGET INVENTORY

Issue: _____

	MY SIDE	**THEIR SIDE**

Positions: _____   _____

_____   _____

_____   _____

_____   _____

_____   _____

_____   _____

_____   _____

Interests: _____   _____

_____   _____

_____   _____

_____   _____

_____   _____

_____   _____

_____   _____

Date: _____

Who Is at the Table . . .
Who Is Not?

Who is on each side of the negotiation table is important. Who is *not* there is also important. Those who are not there, but who have a real stake in the outcome, are ghosts at the table: They may not be there, but they loom over and sometimes dominate the proceedings. Their views must be accounted for and their interests advanced just as much as if they were sitting beside you or across from you.

NEGOTIATING IN TEAMS: NO MORE DAVID AND GOLIATH

Throughout history, champions have frequently been sent to work out conflicts between groups. They were chosen for their special "negotiating" skills. The Philistines chose Goliath as their champion to work on their issues with the Israelites because he was so big and strong. David came forward for the Israelites because everyone else was afraid of Goliath. David had courage and he had a plan. The two nations relied on David and Goliath to solve their problems.

Likewise, in the old days of business, champions also met to hash out problems and make deals for their companies. The champions were typically the owners of the businesses. There were strong advantages to these one-on-one negotiations. The owners knew their businesses and knew what they wanted. They also had the power to make a deal at the table. They didn't have to check with anyone. If something went awry after the agreement was struck, there was just one person to see: the one who made the deal. Simple, straightforward.

Today, most of the time, business is too complex for deals to be cut by two people at a table. It is true that sometimes companies will employ agents, outsiders with special skills, to represent them. Sometimes this is effective. But, sometimes this becomes a process of one-upsmanship, the manipulation of status to gain the upper hand: My negotiator can beat up your negotiator. Even if a gunslinger is brought in for reasons of skill and expertise, he or she frequently operates in concert with a team from the company. Teams are now the order of the day.

THE CHALLENGES OF TEAM NEGOTIATING

Team negotiating, though, presents significant challenges. First, you have to decide who is going to be on the team; and there are many factors to consider:

- The expertise required at the meeting
- The authority of those attending
- The history some may have with those on the other side
- The opportunity cost to other company projects by the time required of the participants
- The personalities of the prospective team members
- The company politics

Assembling the team can be an emotionally charged negotiation in and of itself.

When such an ad hoc team is assembled, it is immediately confronted with the next challenge—a challenge most team members do not usually recognize. At the initial meeting of the team, most of the members focus on the negotiation that is going to be coming up with the other side. Actually, this meeting (and probably subsequent ones) is a negotiation among those who are on the same side. True, the members have many shared interests, but it is no less true that there are divergent perceptions about what is going on, divergent goals, divergent values, and divergent interests among team members.

Like Shakespeare's *Hamlet,* which contains a play within the play, with teams there is a negotiation within a negotiation. Before and during the actual negotiation with the other side, there is negotiation with those on the same side. Failure to recognize this dynamic can produce less than optimal results in other-side negotiations.

When your ad hoc team is assembled, besides recognizing that you are already in a negotiation with your own people, recognize that it will probably be unclear who is going to do what during the negotiation with the other side. Will there be a leader? Will there be someone who will take notes? A listener? A provocateur? Recognize that the participants will likely have differing assumptions about who is going to do what. There will be a premium on clarifying roles.

Know, too, that there may well also be no clearly perceived and commonly understood purpose or set of purposes for either the meetings prior to the other-side negotiation or for the negotiation itself. There may be more divergent than convergent views about goals. Clarifying desired outcomes will be everyone's responsibility.

Further, there will likely be no pre-agreed-on process to establish roles and clarify goals, and this lack of agreement will complicate putting an effective team together.

STREET-SMART REALITY
TEAM NEGOTIATING

Judy is a provider representative for a large health insurance company. Her boss has asked her to assemble a team to negotiate rates for process and procedures with a large network of medical practitioners, a multispecialty group. The group is attached to a teaching hospital in a major metropolitan area, and the rates of the individual doctors, in part because of a predilection among them to experiment and aggressively refer to other specialists, are high. Judy's boss has directed her to assemble a team to negotiate with the docs and to bring the rates down.

Judy has asked Ian, who is an IT specialist, to be on the team, because the company hopes to bring the network on-line with its billings. She has also contacted Fred to be on the team, because he knows some of the doctors and was involved in the last negotiation, which went fairly well from the company's point of view. Rounding out the team is Jill, who is a specialist in the state law and regulations in the jurisdiction where the network and the teaching hospital are located. Jill actually ranks above Judy on the company organization chart.

The team is having its first meeting.

Jill speaks first: "I think we should determine who is going to be the spokesman when we meet with the doctors."

Judy thinks, but does not say, "There she goes trying to be the top dog."

"Why don't we decide first how we are going to proceed here today?" Ian asks.

Fred thinks, but does not say, "Ian must have a better idea of what our purpose is than I do because he is already talking about how to get there."

There you have it. Confusion and varying assumptions about roles, process, and purpose are further exacerbated by statements that are inferred to mean something different from the speaker's intent. Judy, for example, interprets Jill's statement about role clarification to be about hierarchy and probably closes her mind to much of what Jill has to say. All of this confusion is even murkier because it is shot through with the emotions of everyone involved.[2]

Building and directing a negotiation team is a tough job.

DISADVANTAGES OF TEAM NEGOTIATING

Even though team negotiating is commonplace, there are some disadvantages to the team approach you should beware of.

If your team is too big, for example, you may intimidate and put off your opponents. Or, the size may simply hinder its effective operation. A big team can create confusion, and it gives the other side the opportunity to create dissension among your team members.

An additional disadvantage inherent in the team approach is that with more people involved there is a greater chance that people problems will crop up: personality conflicts, bad history, insensitive communications, and conflicts in perceptions. And, of course, these people problems can happen among team members themselves as well as with those on the other side.

ADVANTAGES OF TEAM NEGOTIATING

As your team walks into the negotiating room, you have a number of things going for you.

Psychologists tell us, and my experience makes me believe, that the team, collectively, is smarter than the smartest member of the team. The whole is greater than the sum of the parts. Plus, with a team you have a chance to pick members who have the expertise required to bring your negotiation to a successful conclusion. There is less chance to get hung up on a technical issue.

Teams also provide mutual support for each member. You've got allies there who will back up the things you say. As a group, you have a chance to make a show of strength. Properly assembled, you can appear to the other side as a collective Goliath.

Also, and this is one of the top advantages of a team approach, you can divide the labor of the negotiation. One or more of your team, for example, can be designated a listener. This is important, because if you are talking or preparing to say something in response to something that has been said, but your opposite number is still making points, you are not listening as well as you could be. Additionally, different people hear the same thing differently, and it is good to get another read on what has been said or done.

GHOSTS AT THE TABLE: WHO IS NOT THERE

You cannot, of course, take everyone you would like with you to your negotiation. Many times you cannot take some who could be very important to the negotiation. The person with the ultimate authority to make the deal may not be there. In some circumstances it may be tactically wise to leave the decision maker at home so that you can step away from the deal and have a higher authority take a look at what you're doing before it is a done deal. But, more often than not, the decision maker isn't there simply because of the press of other business.

There are many others with stakes in the outcome who cannot be present: your boss, shareholders, boards of directors, families of participants, those charged with executing any deal that is made. All of these people can be affected by what you do. These are the ghosts at the negotiating table, and their interests must be accommodated.

The same is true on the other side of the table. Your opposites are being affected by their absent stakeholders, and you should do your best to determine the interests of those absent parties, because their interests will help shape the contours of what the other side is saying and doing.

Ask yourself: Who isn't here who has an interest in the outcome? One way to do this is to probe members of the other side about the limit of their authority. Can those present make a deal?

If they candidly admit they cannot, what is your response? Or, perhaps a more delicate question: What if they say they can make a deal, but you have reason to believe they really don't have the authority? What do you do?

WHO'S AT THE TABLE? AND WHO ISN'T?

When I was borrowing money to build nursing homes, this authority issue came up every time I sat down with a lending officer of a bank or an insurance company. It even came up once when I was dealing with the mayor of a small town whose influence I needed to persuade his town council to pass a bond issue for one of my facilities.

In each of these cases I asked the person if he had authority to make a deal, or was there someone besides him I needed to talk to? In every case the response was about the same: "Of course, I can." Or, "No, you're looking at the guy you need to talk to."

Invariably, however, at the end of what was always a protracted and tortuous process, as we congratulated ourselves on getting the deal done, the lender would say something like "All we have to do is run this by the loan committee" (or attorneys, who would make a goal line stand to keep me from advancing my business ball across the goal line). "Please know this is a mere formality. My recommendations have not been turned down in all the years I have been here."

Guess what? My deal would be the first in all his years. Now, most of the time they didn't flat turn down the deal the loan officer and I had negotiated. But the committee or the lawyers would tweak the good deal we negotiated to make it "better."

The tweaking, it may not surprise you, was never to my benefit. They never came back and said, "We are charging you too many points." Or, "This interest rate is usurious. It must come down."

No, their proposals always involved due-on-sale provisions or additional collateral, or higher rates and more points. One savings-and-loan committee even wanted a $50,000 "processing" fee if another entity assumed my mortgage, even if that entity were the United States government.

I needed a séance to speak with the ghosts at the table! How did I deal with this appeal-to-a-person-not-at-the-table tactic? I never found a way that was consistently successful, but one thing I said at times like these had a salutary effect and from time to time kept the loan committee's hands off the deal we had made. I would say, "Oh, I realize in an organization this size you have to have someone reviewing what you do. You have to have checks and balances. But you tell your good people that if they seek to improve what we have done here, I am not going to negotiate with you just on their 'improvement.' The whole deal will be back on the table, and meanwhile, though I want to do the deal with your bank, I am going down the street and see what First National will do."

By the time I ran into the mayor and the city council on the bond issue deal, I had some experience, so I didn't rely completely on what the mayor had told me ("Don't worry, Lacey, we've got the votes"). I knew there were interests in addition to his that I must uncover and accommodate.

The county in which I proposed building this nursing home had the highest unemployment rate in the state. Those folks needed the 100 jobs I was going to bring to the community. But the council members were nervous about encumbering the city's credit by issuing more than $2 million in bonds. Instead of putting all my bets on the mayor, I spent weeks leading up to the vote canvassing the community and generating support by holding out the prospect of jobs and economic growth for the area and by defusing the credit issue. (The city's credit is typically not affected by issuing industrial revenue bonds.) I also spent time with council members individually, but they were largely noncommittal.

> **LESSON FROM THE STREET #26**
>
> If you don't identify the ghosts at the table, they'll come back to haunt you.

As a former state senator, however, I knew something about what moves an elected official.

The night of the meeting, I packed the hall with nearly 100 people, and, after my presentation to the mayor and council, I asked for everyone who supported the bond issue to stand. The whole crowd stood and cheered. The bond issue resolution was passed without a dissenting vote— even though none of the council members had been present when I got my commitment from the mayor and none had made a commitment to me privately. We built the nursing home and the city got more than 100 new jobs.

Beware of the interests of absent parties—both on your side and the other. Take these interests into account, and the ghosts at the table will not cause you fear and trembling. They'll be like Casper—friendly.

————

Where Should You Negotiate . . .
Your *Querencia* or Mine?

Go to Madrid in the late spring to see the bullfights. If you have not been before, you may be surprised by what happens at the beginning.

The bull rushes into the ring. He runs around the arena and stops. He paws the ground. He snorts at the crowd as it roars. His would-be tormentors, attired in brilliant, skin-tight costumes, have yet to get his attention. The matador's *cuadrilla* (assistants) shout and wave their *capotes* (capes) of raw silk and percale, cerise on one side and yellow on the other. The bull may look their way but he is, for now, not interested. He couldn't care less. The crowd of 50,000 screams to approve his nonchalance.

Then, the bull moves around the ring, sometimes slowly, sometimes at a trot. He may or may not approach the bullfighters—the bandrillos, the picadors, and the matador himself. Most of the time, he looks for a spot in the big ring that, for reasons known only to him, he favors. He stays there, and that is where the drama of the fight is played out. He has found his *querencia* (place). He is comfortable there. There he will do his damage, if any he does. There he will meet his fate.

People, like the bull, prefer to conduct business, resolve conflicts, make deals, and negotiate in a place where they are comfortable. They seek their querencia. Most often their querencia is their office. This is where they spend most of their time. This is where their information, their data, is. This is where they can garner support from their allies. This is their comfort zone, and they consider that a great advantage. Sometimes it is.

Sometimes, however, much can be gained by going to the office of the other side.

First, in their querencia, those on the other side can be expected to be most relaxed and at ease. This can work very much to your advantage.

A relaxed person is more open to ideas, suggestions, and opposing views than one who is nervous and uptight because of an unfamiliar environment.

Second, if you go to their office you have a good chance to build rapport. Are pictures of their family on display? Do they have pictures of themselves on the ski slopes or on the tennis court? Do they have framed civic awards on the wall? What about diplomas? Where did they go to school?

What, if any, inference can you draw from their office about their place in the pecking order at the company?

Also, at their office you have more control over the duration of the meeting. At your place, if they drag the conference on by raising "just one more point" and they won't leave your office, it will be hard for you to bring matters to a close. If they are particularly insistent, you either have to kick them out or leave your own office to bring the meeting to an end.

> **LESSON FROM THE STREET #27**
>
> Where should you negotiate? Where most of the parties are most comfortable.

If you feel uncomfortable or at a disadvantage by meeting at their place of suggestion, then try to meet where you feel comfortable or at a neutral site. Wherever the meeting, if you feel uncomfortable, you are at a double disadvantage: Your discomfort keeps you from being at your best, and, in turn, your discomfort will make others uncomfortable. This impedes an open atmosphere for problem solving.

When Should You Negotiate . . . Expedite or Delay?

The *when* of negotiating encompasses more than mere considerations of what month, what day, and what time. It includes issues of pacing, sequencing, rhythm, and deadlines, and these issues have more to do with the *why* and *how* of negotiations. It may be sufficient to say at this point that unless you are involved in a transaction in which it is advantageous to drag matters out because those on the other side face a deadline, I believe you should move to and through your negotiation with all deliberate speed. I've never been a blacksmith, but the admonition "strike while the iron is hot" makes a lot of sense to me.

If you have done your homework, your data is up to date, and the matter is a priority, do it now.

It may seem axiomatic, but preparation is the foundation of success in persuasion. It is almost impossible to overprepare. So give yourself enough time, and prepare.

PREPARE SOME MORE TO GET IT!

The Why and How of Persuasion

The *why* and *how,* mentioned at the beginning of Chapter 4, are shorthand for questions of strategy and tactics in persuasion.

Strategies . . . and Tactics

A strategy is your plan. A tactic is what you do to achieve that plan. Your tactics depend, in part, on what others do in response to you as you work that plan. In the beginning, you plot out what you think is the best course of action (strategy). As you pursue this course of action, the steps you take (tactics) will be affected by the responses of everyone else involved. Their responses are their tactics.

The situation is dynamic. You may plan a certain set of steps to get to your goal, but, as you take those steps, others react to you. You learn *ex post* what you could only guess at *ex ante.* You may change direction. You may drop your plan altogether. You are *not* baking a cake. You are creating something and learning as you go.

In the dance of persuasion there are all sorts of steps, moves, and protocols. After a good bit of sashaying around the floor, with concessions given on all sides, someone may well say, "Wha d'ya say we split the difference?" No matter how many times you hear this proposal, it always has a seductive ring, doesn't it? Why is this?

STREET-SMART REALITY
SPLITTING THE DIFFERENCE

You are the CFO of a small construction company. You and your boss have agreed to add six cars to your fleet for the use of your recently expanded sales force, and the two of you have set a target price of $14,000 per additional car. You will make the buy and you have some latitude to deal. A car at the third dealer you visit catches your eye. It has a $19,000 sticker price—beyond your company target. But you stand there admiring this pile of metal, and a salesman approaches.

"She is a beauty, isn't she? Go ahead; slip into the driver's seat and get a feel for her.

"A good feel, right? You look great behind the wheel."

"Nice car but more than I want to pay."

"Hey, we have a big inventory of these, and I know I could get you out the door for $18,000. Can you handle that?"

"I was looking more at about $13,000." (You don't want to give him too much accurate information.)

"Whoa, we're way off there. But I'll tell you what, let me go talk to my manager and see what I can do."

You see the two men talking with great animation. You suspect they are talking ball scores.

The salesman comes back with a big smile.

"Boy, John is in a good mood today. He says I can let this one on the floor go for $17,500."

Two, you think, can play this game.

"Let me check something. Is there a phone I can use?"

In the cubicle to which he ushers you, you suspect the phone is bugged, but you call and check your messages.

"I can stretch to $14,000, and, by the way," you tell him now, "we are looking to buy six of these if we can buy them right."

"I know we can't do even six for $14,000, but I like that volume and we may be able to do something. Look around and see if there is another car more in your range. Here is my card."

You start for the door.

"Wait a minute. I hate to see you walk out of here. We want to be your car company. What if I could get John to go for $17,000 for the six?"

"Well, I could possibly go to $15,000." There is a long pause.

"Hey, we're just $2,000 apart. Wha d'ya say we split the difference at $16,000, if I can talk John into it and you buy all six today?"

What do you do? Does this seem fair? At $16,000 you are $2,000 above your target, but the dealer has come down from $19,000—$3,000 below sticker.

Why is the salesman's proposal to split the difference at least somewhat appealing? One reason, of course, is that splitting the difference seems fair, on the surface at least. Another reason the proposal has appeal is that in this dance of persuasion you have both made concessions. Concession making engenders a sense of reciprocity, and a proposal to bridge the final gap by meeting halfway, in the context of this reciprocity, is tempting. Also, in this country at least, anything that can be viewed as 50-50 may seem equitable.

> **LESSON FROM THE STREET #29**
>
> Don't split the difference just because it seems fair. The result should get you where you want to go.

But beware. Splitting the difference makes sense only if the result takes you where you want to go. Such a proposal—whether you make it or someone else does—is fair only if the result reflects the value of the thing being bargained over. At the end of your ballet with the car salesman, splitting the difference, in other words, is fair only if $16,000 is the value of the car and you are willing to pay that amount.

———

Another tactic, so timeworn that it is a cliché, relates to the perception of scarcity and the possibility that if you don't act quickly you will lose out. Just because this tactic is a cliché, however, doesn't mean it's not effective. We live in a world of clichés.

[STREET-SMART REALITY]
THE SCARCITY TACTIC

If you are looking to buy a house, at some point the seller or the seller's agent will say, "I'm not trying to pressure you, but I showed the house yesterday to a couple who are very interested. The wife loved it, and I think they are going to make an offer today or tomorrow."

Oldest trick in the book? Perhaps. But it still works on the most sophisticated of us. It gets our adrenaline pumping: "I better act or that couple will buy the house out from under me."

What prescription is there to cure the negotiation malady this tactic can produce in you? Don't fall in love with just one house. Or one anything. Except maybe your partner. Otherwise, have a Plan B.

> **LESSON FROM THE STREET #30**
>
> Except for your partner, don't fall in love with just one thing. Have a Plan B.

We make concessions as a tactic to persuade others because we hope to gain something in return, and we hope to keep the negotiation alive so we can make a deal. This process of giving and taking began with our ancestors. For thousands of years we hunted for food to survive. Our ancient ancestors could not hunt or gather food alone. The environment was too harsh, the dangers too great. Their success depended on cooperation and collaboration, give and take among the members of the tribe. The most collaborative were the most successful. They survived and thus contributed to the gene pool. We have their DNA.

[STREET-SMART REALITY]
ONE HAND WASHING THE OTHER

When I traveled to New York during my years in the coal business, I stayed at a small hotel in mid-Manhattan. The concierge knew every ticket broker, restaurateur, and club owner in town. He could get you what you wanted.

Anthony did me a lot of favors, and, to express my gratitude for his help through the years, I invited him and his wife to Florida, where I was living. They came and we had a great time.

More than a year later, a group of Spanish coal buyers met me in New York and they insisted on eating at Le Cirque, booked in those days, as now, months in advance. I contacted my concierge friend, and he called Serio and got us reservations for eight, including my friend the concierge and his wife.

At the end of a memorable meal I signaled for the check. I knew it would be a whopper. "It's on the house," the waiter said. I looked at my friend.

LESSON FROM THE STREET #31

Without give and take, nothing would ever get done.

"I send a lot of business to this restaurant," he said.

A successful evening was made even better by that wonderful human lubricant, reciprocity.

———

Compromise and concession making are highly effective tactics of persuasion. Some believe lying and bluffing are even more effective.

STREET-SMART REALITY
TACTICAL MISDIRECTION

"Look like the innocent flower, but be the serpent under't."[1] That's the tactical advice Lady Macbeth imparted to her husband. He took it and became king. But uneasy lies the head that wears the crown, and Macbeth soon lost his—head and crown.

In persuading others, is it wise (or ethical)—or is it effective—to appear to be one thing or say one thing to accomplish your ends when actually you are or mean something entirely different?

———

Black Lies . . .
White Lies

The nuns at St. Cecilia's grade school taught us that there were two kinds of sin: mortal and venal. Each had its own set of consequences and each possessed different requirements for its expiation. So, too, in efforts to persuade there are two kinds of lies: black and white. And, as with my grade school teachers' characterization of sin, different consequences flow from the employment of these two kinds of misrepresentation.

With respect to your own behavior, let's begin with what would seem to be an easy case.

You are the marketing director for an anti-malaria drug. One of the statistically remote side effects of the drug has been depression. In a small number of cases (forty-eight), those taking the drug have attempted suicide, and twelve have been successful. Does your company have a responsibility, as it attempts to persuade the public to accept the drug and doctors to prescribe it, to disclose this information? Is it sufficient merely for your drug reps to tell the doctors they visit and leave it up to them to inform their patients, while your national advertising omits any mention of this side effect?

LESSON FROM THE STREET #32

Don't confuse tactics and ethics.

As marketing director, you have received the data about the drug's side effects from your R&D people, and you immediately informed top management. Have you fully discharged your responsibility if management subsequently determines that the incidents are not statistically significant and decides not to inform the public? After all, the drug has been approved by the FDA.

The answers to these questions may seem easy. But in an actual situation with facts similar to this hypothetical case, no voluntary disclosure was made to the physicians or to the public by *anyone working for the company.*

It doesn't take long for ethics and tactics to become entwined.

You are looking at an apartment to rent for you and your family. It fits your needs perfectly. Should you try to get a lower rent by saying that it really does not fit your needs but you would be willing to take it if the rent were lower?

Tactical misdirection? Well, consider another situation.

You are the chairman of the local board of health. The mayor comes to you and asks you to help him fire the executive director of the board. You like the director and have a good relationship with her, but you consider her only marginally competent and have wanted her replaced for some time. You've been trying to figure a way to ease her out. You see your opening and say, "I'd really hate to lose Helen, Mr. Mayor. We have an excellent relationship, but I'll tell you what: If you help me get that special appropriation for anthrax testing your office has been sitting on for so long, I think we can work something out regarding Helen."

It's an out-and-out lie but justifiable by the importance of the anthrax testing. Right? Maybe not.

STREET-SMART REALITY
THE HURT FROM TRUTH AND LIES

When I was a state senator, abortion was a big issue. It still is and probably always will be. There is little a state senator can do about abortion except pontificate. That didn't matter, though, to the most vocal opponents of abortion. They wanted me, their senator, to sponsor legislation that would lead to a U.S. constitutional prohibition against abortions of all kinds. This made no sense to me for a lot of reasons, but large numbers of my constituents favored such an amendment.

Confronted by a group of priests, nuns, and Catholic laypeople on the senate floor, I responded to their request to lead the call for a constitutional ban in words something like these: "I am very sympathetic to what you want. You cannot believe how many people approach me about this issue. My own views on abortion are consonant with yours, *and* (notice I did not say "but") we must zealously guard against the government imposing its will upon us in this or any other matter where liberty is at stake."

A little political misdirection, a little fancy footwork, no outright lying, just finesse, and I could go on representing the good people of Kentucky on a wide range of other important issues on which I could actually make a difference.

But as so often is the case, glibness has its price.

As the legislative session came down to its last days and my constituents realized I had not rallied to the cry for a constitutional convention, I began to receive sacks of mail, mostly from schoolchildren in the Catholic parishes of my district, asking for my support and slamming my lack of leadership on so crucial an issue.

Feelings were so intense about this issue that
one of my own party's precinct captains actually spit
on my hand when I tried to shake hers at a picnic.

I looked back on that initial meeting on the senate floor and rued my lack of candor. If I had been
more candid, though I would have earned the
opprobrium of many voters, their expectations of me on the abortion matter would have been lower and my subsequent actions might have been
seen not as a betrayal but merely as misguided wrong-headedness—a
venal but not a mortal sin.

———

At the height of your efforts to persuade someone to do what you want, it
is tempting to shade the truth, to exaggerate, to dissemble. It is a temptation to which we all have succumbed.

So what incentive is there to resist this temptation, or should we be
untroubled by giving in if the result is just a white lie? Does the end jus-
tify the means? After all, others lie to us; and we are at a distinct disadvantage, are we not, if we cannot ourselves lie at least some? This is a tough
question. Whatever your answer, there are many ramifications.

There are ethical considerations, of course. But whatever side you
come down on with respect to ethics, it may be easier to decide what to do
on practical grounds. In matters of persuasion, your credibility is of great
importance to your success. If you are discovered in a lie—even a small
one—everything you say or do will be put in doubt. Your lie becomes like
the clock that strikes thirteen, after which its timekeeping is suspect. You
will not be believed.

Is there any circumstance when you can bend the truth or tactically
misdirect to even the odds without risking your credibility? Is there such a
thing as a white lie, a venal sin, without dire consequences?

STREET-SMART REALITY
"BLABBING" THE TRUTH

Allan Dulles, former director of the CIA, visited Princeton University in
1963. He had operated at the highest levels of our government and was a

familiar figure on the campus. He held office hours and encouraged students to drop in for visits. On one of these visits, a student asked him how he was able to balance the obligation to be truthful in appearing before various committees of the Congress with the necessity to keep confidential certain information that could affect our national interest, even declassified information, which is nonetheless sensitive.

"I listen very carefully to the question. If I absolutely cannot answer it without disclosing information that could compromise us, I say so. If I can answer, I answer as narrowly as possible. Occasionally, I'll answer a question that has not been asked but may be subsumed by the question actually asked. But generally, I try to follow the advice I give my associates: be truthful, but you don't have to blab the truth."[2]

I think I know what Dulles meant. In the situation involving the rental of the apartment, for example, you should not lie about the space fitting your needs as a stratagem to lower the rent. But you have no obligation to disclose the fact that if you don't rent the apartment today, you and your family will have no place to sleep tonight.[3]

Not telling the whole truth, omitting some material fact, can also amount to a lie, of course. Whether such omission amounts to a lie or not becomes a matter of opinion. But what Dulles said may be a useful guideline: Tell the truth but don't blab it.

Or you can characterize what you say—that which is not entirely true—as "tactical misdirection," and a lie becomes more palatable, at least to you.

The extent to which you bend the truth is a matter of judgment and ethics. Just remember the thirteenth chime of the clock. It's your decision.

> **LESSON FROM THE STREET #34**
>
> Don't lie, but don't blab the truth either.

———

Lies have consequences, and your credibility is at risk even with a tactical misdirection. But, again, you have no obligation to blab the truth.

The extent to which others lie to you is, of course, their decision. You can, however, influence their lying, and you can minimize its negative effect on you.

Sometimes it's easy to spot a lie because it's what Huckleberry Finn called a "stretcher." The premise is so preposterous that it could not be true.

"Our coal has never been out of spec."

"The loan committee always accepts my recommendations."

The inapt choice of words gives it away: "never," "always." Or, the context in which an averment is made can indicate that what is being said is very likely wrong.

"We expect our profits to exceed last year's" (during an economic downturn when profits throughout the industry are plummeting).

Words...
and the Level of Events

Another good way to spot a lie is to compare for consistency what is said with what is done.

A contractor proposing to work on your house tells you "Give me a down payment of $4,000, and I'll be willing to jump off a bridge for you. By tonight, I'll have all your electrical fixtures picked up from Home Depot and delivered to your house, so the electrician can start installation tomorrow."

You give him a check and then don't see him for two days and can't get him on the phone. No matter what reason he gives you for nonperformance, when he asks for money next time, he should be paid for what he has *done,* not what he is *going to do.*

Don't completely discount what is said. But operate on the level of events—what is happening—and not only on what is said.

Recent research suggests that with training and practice you can learn to read the micro-expressions on a person's face and know what is in his mind. If this is true, such training will give pioneer practitioners a great advantage in negotiation and persuasion. In time, of course, as the knowledge of this process becomes widespread, techniques to defeat it will arise. Congenital liars will learn to manage their expressions, micro and macro, much as some, with practice, can fool the polygraph.

Staunch apostles of these new face-reading techniques argue, however, that there are some facial expressions that you cannot fake. They are involuntary. Certain kinds of lying may become obsolete.

From preliminary indications, bluffing is not a likely candidate for obsolescence. So how do you deal with someone who says she will or won't do something (won't come down in her asking price or up with her offer), and you are not sure she has communicated her reservation price, her best offer?

Short of mind reading or taking the course in micro-expression reading, the best way to discover reality is by asking carefully crafted questions, tactful but probing.

You must be certain that your questions do not permit the inference that you believe the bluffer may be lying. You should not say, "Hey, you said before you'd be finished for sure by the first; now you are saying the fifteenth. What's up with that?"

Rather, you should say, "The fifteenth. Hey, that's my daughter's birthday. Why do you think you can finish by then?" Don't even mention the previous projection of the first. Then, listen carefully. What is said next will probably tell you whether the fifteenth will also be a missed completion date.

What if the bluffer says, "If you can't get your corporate folks to approve our offer of settlement by two weeks from today, the offer is off the table, and we'll just have to see you in court"?

In this situation, one tactic would be to ignore what is said, try to get the settlement offer approved (if it's acceptable to you), and if the two weeks come and go and you still don't have corporate approval, see what the bluffer does. You can still settle after a suit is filed.

Or, if you don't want to risk putting in all the effort, falling short by a day or two, and losing the offer, you should try the tactful question: "Two weeks and the offer expires? Talk to me about how you came up with two weeks. What kind of time pressures are your people under?" Notice I did not say, "What kind of pressure are *you* under?" Such personalization might put the bluffer on the defensive.

> **LESSON FROM THE STREET #35**
>
> Don't rely on words. Operate on the level of events. Verify with tactful questions.

At this point, something may be revealed about the two-week time limit that could help you help them. The bluffer answers your question: "In two weeks our basis point commitment from our fund source will change, and with our costs likely to go up we won't be able to offer you our current figure."

This information gives you something to work with, doesn't it? You can make a contingent commitment keyed to any change in the basis point situation if you are unable to get an answer in two weeks and the rate changes. You may be able to adjust what your company can pay and keep the potential deal in play even after the two-week deadline. Remember: In matters of *tactics,* bluffing may be uncovered by *tactful* questions. "Tactics" and "tactful," after all, share common Latin and Greek roots.

I'm Committed . . .
You're Committed

Convincing the other side that you are committed to a course of action and, its twin, getting the other side firmly committed to a course of action—these are the most potent strategies you can employ in answering the *why* and *how* of your persuasions and negotiations.

Convincing is tricky. Most of the time, your commitments and those of the folks across from you are expressed in words; and words may be discounted, and they have an evanescent quality. They can fade fast.

In the world of the *Godfather* movies, you would be believed if you swore on the heads of your children or, if childless, your mother. As a child, you could cross your heart and hope to die. But in our world there are no magic words to convince others that we mean what we say. If there were, we would have great power to persuade, the power of belief.

Short of magic, there are ways to convince others that we mean what we say. Like most worthwhile things, it takes a little work and a little creativity.

In the theater there is a convention or device known as *deus ex machina,* which literally means god from a machine. By employing this device, the playwright saves what appears to be a hopeless situation for the protagonists by the introduction of a surprising, if often unbelievable, external force. The Greeks, whose religion provided them an easy excuse, would simply solve a problem in a dramatic production by bringing in a god. In movies of the past, the classic example of this device is the arrival, just in time, of the U.S. Cavalry to save the settlers from certain death at the hands of marauding Indians.

In persuasion, the use of something from the outside, something external, can rid your words of their ephemeral quality and can convince people you mean what you say.

STREET-SMART REALITY
DEUS EX MACHINA

A particularly contentious legal battle was being waged in circuit court. Neither side would consider seriously the reasonable offers of the other to settle. The court was deluged with motions and petitions. After months of presiding over this wrangling, the judge called the attorneys to his chambers.

"Folks, this lawsuit is taking on the dimensions of *Jarndyce v. Jarndyce*" (the case in Charles Dickens's *Bleak House* that lasted generations), "and I want to tell you something that under ordinary circumstances I would not bring into the courtroom. I have been diagnosed with throat cancer. I begin chemo in three weeks at the Mayo clinic. I have asked you to bring me a reasonable settlement—and we all know one is possible—and now I am strongly suggesting that you bring me one in the twenty-one days before I go to Minnesota, or your clients will face starting over with a new judge."

The proposed settlement was on his desk the next week. Everyone knew the judge meant what he said. An external power lent veracity to his words, a veracity that was unquestionable. It's hard to argue with cancer. *Deus ex machina.*

THE POWER OF COMMITMENT

You may not have at hand an external force to convince someone that you are bound to what you say. I use this example, though, to illustrate the fact that perhaps the most effective way to constrain or cause another to act is to show them that you yourself are irrevocably committed and that you cannot withdraw that commitment.

I was introduced formally to the concept of irrevocable commitment in law school. Professor James Vorenberg said on the first day of our course in Corporations: "A corporation is a legal person with the power to sue and be sued."

I presumed that a corporation had the power to sue because I read about such suits in the *Wall Street Journal* nearly every day. But the *power* to be sued? Why was being able to be sued a power? I thought a power was something good, and being sued, to me, did not fall into the good category.

I realized in time that the power to be sued is the power to commit, and without this power to commit and bind itself legally, with legal consequences, a corporation would not be able to find anyone who would do business with it. By doing business, the corporation irrevocably commits itself to the legal consequences of its acts. By incorporating under the laws of any state, the business entity says to the world, "You may deal with us and know that if we don't live up to our commitments you have clear means of redress in the courts of this state."

A-line-in-the-sand tactic is a form of this irrevocable commitment.

Recently, the income for a major metropolitan orchestra declined so much that the organization faced bankruptcy. Reviewing possible options, the orchestra manager said to a newspaper reporter, "I refuse to reduce the size of the orchestra as an option. I would have to leave if that happened."

Here is a clear line in the sand. Or to change the metaphor, the manager has clearly painted himself in a corner. No matter what, he will not be part of reducing the number of players to cut costs. Before that public statement, he could have advanced the idea of a smaller ensemble, or he could have accepted that provision as part of a larger compromise. Now he has surrendered the power to accept that provision. But by doing so, he has created power. The board will have to be willing to see him go if they vote for a smaller operation. For him, this is a risky line in the sand.

Another way to be convincing is to have great credibility based on what you have done in the past. If Jim Smith told a farmer in the coalfields, "Johnny, that price is about the best I can do," the farmer believed him. The farmer knew Jim had thought about it, considered the price fair, and had the power to write a check. Commitment.

RAPPORT AND CONFIRMATION

Rapport is a great help too. The more rapport you have with the other side, the easier it is to convince them that your "best" offer really is your best offer.

Rapport gets you in the door and can help see you through tough times in a bargaining relationship. But rapport will take you only so far. Confirmation is important.

Say you owe $250,000 on a piece of property that is worth at least that much. You will go broke if you don't get what you owe when you sell the property, so a prospective buyer, if convinced of your situation, knows that he'll have to pay you at least the $250,000 to get you to let it go. Confirmation of your financial circumstance from a third source helps the buyer realize you aren't kidding when you say you've got to have at least $250,000. It would also help if the prospective buyer could confirm from an independent source that you had, say, turned down an offer of $240,000.

> **LESSON FROM THE STREET #36**
>
> The power to commit yourself gives you the power to convince and persuade.

Words in Ink . . .
Words in the Air

Although it seems obvious, something commonly overlooked is the fact that you should write down what is said during efforts to persuade—especially efforts that take place over more than one meeting. These notes, while they are not commitments or agreements, can be helpful in reminding everyone involved, including most notably, perhaps, yourself, of what has been committed to, even if only conditionally.

This is particularly the case once an agreement has been reached. The more quickly you get it down on paper the better. You may be able to rely on the word of those with whom you are dealing, but you cannot rely on their memories.

———

STREET–SMART REALITY
GETTING IT IN WRITING NO MATTER WHAT

When the West Louisville Boys' Choir returned from their tour of Europe, they gave a concert for those who had contributed money for the tour.

When the boys sang their last song, a moving rendition of "Amazing Grace," the University of Louisville president, John Shumaker, who had helped raise the money for the tour, made an astonishing announcement.

"Boys, we need to do more than just send you to Europe, bring you back to a big party, and send you home. I'll say this to you: If you stay in the choir, graduate from high school, and get admitted to the University of Louisville, I'll guarantee you a full four-year scholarship so you can get a college degree!"

His words stunned the audience—but not as much as the boys in the choir—for most of whom, minutes earlier, "college" had been just a word in the dictionary.

For weeks after his announcement, those of us close to the choir wallowed in a kind of aftershock of self-congratulatory bliss. Then the morning newspaper dealt us a shock. Its headline announced that John had been chosen president of the University of Tennessee. The choir's chief benefactor was moving.

I try to be a student of my own teaching, so I made an appointment with the outgoing president and his interim replacement for the purpose of getting in writing the university's commitment to the choir. I asked for the interim president, Carol Garrison, to be there to assure some continuity and support of the commitment. We got a letter with the outgoing president's signature and the interim president as a witness.

I felt comfortable now, particularly because I thought the interim president had a fair chance of becoming the permanent president.

Then came shock number two. Carol was moving to the University of Alabama at Birmingham.

A new interim president was chosen. I called for an appointment. My purpose? To inform him personally of the university's commitment to the choir and the reasons for it. The executive assistant to the president, who had also been John's executive assistant, told me the new president was very busy but that he had been made aware of the commitment to the choir and that he supported it.

Meanwhile, the governor announced a state revenue shortfall for the coming fiscal year, which would cause several million dollars to be cut from the university budget.

Should I write the new president? His response would surely reconfirm the commitment, but I didn't want to risk getting something in writing as a response that could weaken what I had—a commitment, for example, conditioned on the availability of revenue after the state budget cuts. If, on the other hand, the university's commitment could become more widely known, it would pick up support. A news story about the wonderful promise to the boys could help. The article appeared. The public response was strong. The scholarship program became well known throughout the community and was even mentioned from the pulpit of several churches.

In the first two years after the program was announced, four students from the choir benefited from the scholarship program at the university. Five applied in the third year, and all met the requirements and were expected to enroll.

The lesson to me from this experience is that the more you memorialize the commitments others make to you, and the more third-party support you can generate for them, the better chance you have that the promises will be kept. At a minimum, get it in writing.

The United States Marine Corps has a powerful method of enforcing the promises of its recruits. When a recruit breaks a rule or fails to meet a benchmark, the price or punishment is levied not just on the recruit but on the entire platoon. A recruit may tolerate the personal punishment and repeat an offense, but it is harder when the other recruits will also be punished because of his or her unacceptable behavior.

———

In sum, the strategic key to making lasting agreements is to make any deal you strike self-executing or so painful to break that keeping it is easier than breaking it.

PART THREE

HOW THREE EMOTION-PACKED SKILLS GET IT!

POCKET THE CURRENCY OF EMPATHY

The Heads Side of the Human Connection Coin

Empathy makes rapport possible. Rapport can begin and/or sustain a relationship. Together, empathy and rapport form the two-sided coin of human connection. Pocket this coin and you maximize your chance to persuade.

Start with empathy.

What It Is . . .
What It Isn't

Empathy. You hear and see this word a lot. What does it mean? Why is it a good thing? Let's see first what it isn't.

Empathy is not compassion. You feel compassion for someone who deserves help—maybe from you, but certainly from somebody. Your neighbors' son loses his college scholarship because family income has risen, not enough to make much difference, but enough to disqualify him from assistance. You feel compassion for the family.

Empathy is not sympathy, though it sounds like it. If you sympathize with someone, you feel sorry for them. Your co-worker misplaces an important document. She is distraught. You are sympathetic.

Empathy is not pity. Pity involves feeling sorry for someone, like sympathy; but pity also involves your judging the person you pity for putting themselves in the situation they're in. The hothead at work loses his temper once too often and is passed over for his long-expected promotion. He is a victim of his own shortcoming. You pity him.

Nor is empathy merely feeling what someone else is feeling, although that can be part of it. When President Clinton said, "I feel your pain," he was being, if sincere, empathic on one level. But feeling what someone is feeling doesn't really amount to much if it stops there. Nor is merely recognizing what someone is feeling, even if you don't feel it yourself, a good working definition of empathy—if recognizing what they feel is all that you do.

STREET–SMART REALITY
KNOWING WHAT THEY FEEL, FEELING WHAT THEY FEEL

When I was a young man, my friend Marvin carried a knife so big you could see its outline where the ends of the knife had worn through and made white spots on the pocket of his blue jeans.

Mostly, he kept the knife in his pocket, but when we were around girls he had a favorite way of showing off with it. Clearing away the drinks and glasses on the table, he would fish out the knife, snap open its blade, put his left palm flat in the clearing on the table, spread his fingers, and begin his scary trick. He stabbed the space outside his left little finger with the knife, then the space between the little finger and the next, stabbing between his fingers clockwise until at last he stabbed the table just outside his left thumb. Then, he'd start back counterclockwise, picking up speed as he went. Back and forth he would go, stabbing faster and faster until the girls screamed.

No matter how may times I saw him do this, each time, forcing myself to look because of my own machismo, I would feel the blade, errant at last, strike the knuckle, pierce his freckled finger, split the bone, and pin his hand to the table in a spreading puddle of his blood. It never happened. But I always thought it would, and I could feel it happen every time. Years later, Marvin admitted he could feel it happen sometimes too. On several occasions, I would, out of earshot of the girls, discourage him from pulling his knife trick, but he always did it whenever he got the chance.

> **LESSON FROM THE STREET #38**
>
> Feeling the same emotion as another, or at least recognizing it, is the beginning of empathy.

———

In looking for a good definition of empathy, notice that you may recognize an emotion in another and you may experience that same emotion, but you may have a different feeling.

Confused? This story may clear things up.

STREET-SMART REALITY
SAME EMOTION, DIFFERENT FEELING

Red and his wife, Martha, started a bookstore, Red-Mart, in a community where a store of thirty years standing had just closed. In the beginning they had no competition, and, though short on experience, they flourished.

Red worked the numbers and did the buying, and Martha worked the community, the customers, and the staff. In twenty-five years they built the store to four locations with more than 100 full- and part-time employees. In the most recent five years, though, big-name booksellers came to town. Discount stores began selling hardbacks at steep discounts. Online booksellers cranked up to the point that book buying habits in the community began to change. Then came the straw, the last one, just short weeks after

> **LESSON FROM THE STREET #39**
>
> Empathy has many faces. You may share someone's emotion and not his feelings.

Red-Mart's anniversary party: Another major chain announced it would open an outlet right up the street from Red and Martha's anchor store.

The Saturday following that announcement, Red and Martha assembled their employees and announced they were selling out. All of the employees, some of whom had been there for twenty-five years, from the beginning, cried. Red and Martha cried too.

As Martha watched Red uncharacteristically display his emotions, it occurred to her that while she and Red were both sad, their sadness could not be the same feeling, because their experiences with the store had been so different. Red traveled to conventions, met authors, bought books, saw to the back office, dealt with accountants and with the IRS. And Martha had built up friendships with the staff and the customers and had become a well-known civic figure, almost indistinguishable from her store.

———

A PRACTICAL DEFINITION OF EMPATHY

Empathy is the exercised ability to infer accurately what someone is thinking and feeling over a particular time frame and to act on that inference.

I say "exercised" because possessing the ability to be empathic, as we have seen, doesn't make you that way. And not everyone who has the ability to make accurate inferences about the thoughts and feelings of others actually exercises that ability to good purpose.

And I say "over a particular time frame" because empathy is not a snapshot. It is dynamic, a video of what someone is thinking and feeling.

I also include in the definition of empathy the requirement to "act on the inference." You've got to do something with your insight or it is like a sound with no ears to hear it.

Motivation is a threshold condition for empathy. Explore the reasons for that motivation, and you will have the answer to why empathy is important to you.

EMPATHIC MOTIVATION AT WORK

You may think that if you're the boss, it's not so important to be able to divine the thoughts and feelings of your subordinates. After all, they have to do what you want them to do. Right? You give directions and follow up. They take directions and execute. That's the way it was, maybe, in the late nineteenth and early twentieth centuries, but it's not the way it is today.

STREET-SMART REALITY
EMPATHY AND CLARIFICATION

Steve was part of the management team of a large beverage concern that had decided to contract for the development of new mission and vision statements. The $250,000 price was, they decided, well worth the purpose and direction it would give to this multinational company with several thousand employees.

Two years after the adoption of these "viz/mish" statements, Steve contracted with a consultant to analyze how the statements were being attended to and followed on a daily basis by his reports (12) and by the employees in their charge (6,000). The consultant interviewed each of the managers separately as well as many of those whom they managed. The line workers were without exception unaware of the goals in the statements, nor could any repeat the statements, even in their own words. Most of the managers, while aware of the vision and mission statements, confused their purpose, and there was wide variation in the managers' thoughts about what the statements contained. (The consultant interviewed the managers outside their offices so they could not read the statements, which hung on every office wall.)

This information shocked Steve.

"I shouldn't have to tell someone I am paying more than $200,000 what my feelings and thoughts are about our mission and vision statements!"

"Well, maybe you shouldn't have to tell them. But if you want to make sure they know, you have to tell them, and repeatedly."

The managers at Steve's company didn't have empathic accuracy with Steve on the vision and mission statements. This cost the company money. The line workers couldn't be expected to know how their work furthered the company purpose if their managers didn't have a clear idea themselves. People were working. Everyone was busy. But there was no agreed-on purpose of what all that activity was about.

> ### LESSON FROM THE STREET #40
>
> Accurate empathy requires clarification. Check to make sure you understand what you see and hear and that you have been understood.

Steve didn't know what was on the minds of his managers either—not, that is, until he hired someone to find out. To Steve's credit, at least he knew that he didn't know.

———

EMPATHIC ACCURACY AT HOME

Most people are motivated to be empathic in their personal relationships, especially in the early years of those relationships. Most newlyweds, for example, are acutely attuned to what their spouse is thinking or feeling at a particular time—most but not all.

STREET-SMART REALITY
EMPATHY—ACCURATE AND INACCURATE

The movie *Diner*, a wonderful period piece set in 1959 Baltimore, contains two strong examples of accurate and inaccurate empathy. The story revolves around a group of young male friends who hang out at the Falls Point Diner, a classic chrome art deco structure with red and blue stripes running down its sides. It also involves two of their women. Beth, a new wife, played by Ellen Barkin, is unable to understand how strongly her husband, Shrevie, played by Daniel Stern, feels about his record collection and its filing system. She files a James Brown recording under the "J's" in the rock and roll section instead of under the "B's" in the rhythm and blues section. Shrevie yells that she is not to touch his records ever.

"You don't understand! This is important to me! Every record is associated with an important event in my life."

Beth feels so bad about this fight and its many predecessors that she accepts an invitation to go to bed with Boogie, an old boyfriend (played by Mickey Rourke). The liaison doesn't come off, but you can see what a lack of empathy may lead to.

In contrast, Eddie and Elyse, who are engaged to be married in the movie, demonstrate something about empathy that is worth learning. Eddie (Steve Guttenberg) is a football fan(atic) who wants Elyse (whom we never see) to be well informed about football and all of its arcania before they marry. He feels so strongly about this that he requires Elyse to pass a

140-question test about the sport as a precondition to the marriage. She needs a 65 to pass. The test is really tough. She scores 63.

The wedding is off.

Eddie eventually relents, however. He gives Elyse a "break," mostly because she tried so hard. She knew what was important to Eddie. She was willing to learn about something that she had little interest in because Eddie was interested in it. She was empathic—enough, at least, to identify which rookie held the record for the longest run from scrimmage in his first professional football game (at the time of the movie, Alan the "Horse" Ameche, seventy-nine yards). She got an "A" for effort. She read Eddie's feelings, responded accordingly, and the nuptials went forward.[1]

> **LESSON FROM THE STREET #41**
>
> Empathic accuracy is important. But even if you miss the mark, you can still get an "A" for effort.

When motivation on the part of both sender and receiver is high (newly-weds or newly employed), being empathic is a challenge. When people try to hide what they feel, making accurate inferences is very problematic. Sometimes people don't purposefully try to hide their feelings, but they may be predisposed to do so. They're hardwired like that.

Whether they are operating on evolutionary autopilot or by design, you have to go a step further to determine what's really on someone's mind in these circumstances.

STREET-SMART REALITY
INNATE COMMUNICATIONS

The wasp is the enemy of the caterpillar. And the wasp, for the caterpillar, is not a good enemy to have. The soft, slow-moving caterpillar has no defense of its own against this highly mobile, hostile, winged and stinging, hard-bodied creature.

But the butterfly caterpillar has evolved a marvelous defense to the wasp. The caterpillar has little antennae that project from its head and vibrate with a sound similar to that of an ant hitting the ground with its belly to signal to other ants either danger or the presence of food. Whether for comestibles or conflict, many ants soon congregate around the caterpillar.

Once they are there, the caterpillar has something else to help itself. Behind its head the caterpillar has protrusions that, when a wasp is near, emit a pheromone that for an ant is an alarm chemical. When nearby ants sense the pheromone, they viciously attack the insect threatening their fellow crawler.

Good Samaritan ants? No, the caterpillar has fooled the ant into helping him, and for good measure the caterpillar has given the ant something in return for this protection. In addition to the vibrations and the pheromones, the caterpillar has evolved on its body two tiny saddlebags that, when the ant strokes them, excrete an amino acid that is nutritious for the ant. It's a symbiotic relationship.[2]

This evolutionary symbiosis has meaning for us as we tower above these insects in the grass.

We've mentioned deception and reciprocity, but a broader implication of the studies that inform us about the ants and caterpillars is that all of us who live on this planet have evolved communication systems that are innate—automatic or spontaneous as well as volitional.

Dazzle your friends at a cocktail party with the observation that Charles Darwin was the first to describe this process of emotional communication among animals.[3] Darwin hypothesized that animals are hardwired to communicate many emotions to others without any conscious effort. This is not to say such communications are without purpose. They are not volitional, but they are purposive. The purpose or reason gave rise to the evolutionary development of the particular form of communication.

Animals communicate their feelings. And some of these hardwired communications among animals—birds and mammals—are marked by signs.

It is said, for example, that in the presence of someone attractive, we humans, like the caterpillar but for different reasons, give off pheromones. It happens without our doing anything.

Today, in fact, if you suspect that you have a pheromone deficit—you are not doing well at attracting others—you can buy a little vial of pheromones. Supposedly, with its application you can attract people as a butterfly caterpillar attracts ants.

Other forms of emotional communication also seem to be automatic. When we are sad, for example, certain of our facial muscles behave in a way beyond our control, and we look, among other things, "down in the mouth."

Watch a baby watch its mother. The mother smiles in conversation with a friend. The baby smiles. The mother laughs. The baby laughs. The mother becomes serious, maybe angry, or irritable. The baby begins to fuss.

Practice watching people smile. Try to guess if what they are feeling is really what they are expressing on their face. At first it will be difficult. They're smiling? They're happy. Maybe not. Concentrate. There are certain muscles around our eyes that we cannot make into a smile if we truly are not feeling the emotion that involuntarily produces smiling. It's like trying to rub your stomach and pat your head at the same time. Not impossible. But anyone watching will be amused by your efforts. With practice you'll be able to tell when someone is laughing on the outside but crying on the inside.

> **LESSON FROM THE STREET #42**
>
> People give off signs and signals about their feelings. Some are innate, some volitional. Practice distinguishing them.

This nonvolitional or nonintentional kind of communication between sender and receiver is what social scientists call "veridical." That is, these communications are the most empathically accurate and true because they are pre-attuned in us by the experience of our caveman forebears. It's in our blood. In other words, we cannot manipulate these communications. They are pure.

––––––

It is good to be aware of these veridical signs, because they tell us with certainty something about what is going on in the minds of others, and moreover, perhaps, they tell us how we can affect what is going on there.

There are a number of qualities that you may think affect our ability to be empathic. Some matter more than others. Surprisingly, perhaps, some don't matter at all.

Qualities That Matter . . .
Those That Don't

How is it that some of us can suck up the emotions of others like a vacuum cleaner sucks up dropped kernels of popcorn in a theater after a movie and some of us just never get it?

What characteristics and circumstances permit some to make accurate empathic judgments, like Elyse in *Diner,* while others, like Beth, even when there is a lot at stake, just don't get it? Is it intelligence? Personality? Psychological adjustment? Sensitivity? Socialization? Gender? Context in which empathy is exercised? Skill from practice?

Forget about the first five on the list. At this point, all the research indicates there isn't much difference in empathic ability and accuracy as a function of being smart, having a great personality, being well adjusted, being in touch with your feminine side, or knowing how to play well with others.[4]

GENDER

But what about gender? It has long been believed that women are more empathic than men. This is not just a shibboleth. Some sound research strongly suggests that women can figure out better what is going on in the minds of others than men can.

Women, unlike men, don't have to get in touch with their feminine side. They are feminine. They are more intuitive. They are more collaborative. Many grow up playing games such as jump rope and dolls that require them to take the perspective of others into account. Boys play king of the hill. You don't worry about the feelings of your playmates in this game. You're just trying to knock them off the hill and get to the top yourself.

Deborah Tannen and others have explored gender issues thoroughly with regard to communication styles and what happens in the workplace because of these styles. Much of this research has validated some stereotypes about women.[5] But does it prove they are more empathic than men?

> **LESSON FROM THE STREET #43**
>
> Women are more empathic than men but mainly because they want to be.

Not to me. Some studies, in fact show that while women were better than men at figuring out thoughts and feelings from people's nonverbal behaviors, the results were based primarily on women's skills at decoding intentional facial expressions. When it came to decoding thoughts based on nonfacial clues provided by body language, voice tones, or unintentional micro-expressions, or where there was a conflict between visual and auditory clues, women's empathic superiority dropped off sharply.[6]

Women in the workplace, though, in my experience, consistently show more motivation to care about and find out what others are thinking than men do.

I call this situational disposition rather than an innate pre-attunement. In plain English, women are and have been required by their traditionally subordinate role in the workplace to be very tuned in to what their male superiors and co-workers are thinking and feeling. Their success has depended on the development of this skill. Not so for the male worker. He hasn't had to be so tuned in. At the beginning of the twenty-first century, this is still a fact in workplace America. But it's changing.

CONTEXT

Empathy doesn't occur, nor do you act on it, in a vacuum. There is always a context, an environment, in which it takes place. And the context may well determine how effectively the empathy is deployed, how empathic you are in a given situation.[7]

STREET-SMART REALITY
EMPATHY, CONTEXT, AND DISTRACTION

Cade and Darcy were co-workers on an important company initiative that had a series of time-sensitive benchmarks. Well behind schedule, they agreed to meet in Cade's office after work to try to catch up. Two hours into the work, tired and with nerves on edge, they debated a particularly important decision. The phone rang. Cade was not expecting a call. He had voice mail. On the fourth ring, he picked up the receiver. It was a telemarketer for a credit card company. Darcy exploded and left the office.

Why did Cade answer the phone at such a crucial time in an important face-to-face discussion with someone so potentially crucial to his career? What kind of empathy toward Darcy was he showing?

In forming your answer, consider two situations.

In the first, the setting is a small town. As a shopper emerges from a store on a side street, he sees a man on the ground. It is unclear whether the man requires emergency assistance. He may be drunk. He may be injured. No one else is in sight.

In the second setting a man is on the ground in the street of a major city. Again, the need for emergency aid is unclear. Shoppers emerge from a nearby store. There are many people in the street.

Now, ask yourself: Of the people who see this man in each situation, in the small town and in the big city, what percent would you expect to stop and at least determine if aid is required as they pass by?

Why do you reach these conclusions?

If you assign a high percentage to the Good Samaritans in the small town compared to a small percentage for those in the city, you would be correct but perhaps not for the reasons you may think.

If only a comparatively few of the big-city dwellers stop, despite their greater numbers, it is not because they are more callous, toughened, and anesthetized by the friction of close living. It is because, in the first place, there are so many of them. Responsibility is thereby diffused: I don't have to stop. Someone else will take care of the guy. Plus, when there is a crowd, the individual, for better or worse, does what everyone else is doing. Everyone is stepping over this poor wretch. So will I. Then, too, the big city is so noisy and clamorous, it's easy to be distracted, and it's hard to figure out exactly what's going on in the rich tapestry of the street.

What implications does all of this have for you in your efforts to be empathic and to measure the empathic accuracy of others and thereby take you farther down the road of persuasion?

More than anything, since empathy does not occur in a vacuum, when a situation calls for clearly ferreting out the thoughts and feelings of the people you hope to persuade, you need to eliminate as much distraction as possible and create a context within which you can focus. Even the Good Samaritan in the book of Luke may have behaved differently in a different context. If there had been a lot of people in the street, he may have passed by his unfortunate fellow human being himself. Same Samaritan, different context, different result.

Context is so powerful an influence on empathy that people sometimes create a contextual inference about their feelings as well as the feelings of others that can be completely unwarranted. They create a fact out of their feelings, feelings developed from the context of what is happening.

Susan Clancy, in researching the controversial phenomenon of false memory, has studied women reporting recovered memories of sexual abuse and people who have reported abduction by aliens. In both cases she hypothesized that some people have a tendency to create false memories and that they may be expected to demonstrate this tendency on a standard memory test. This demonstration would permit an evaluation of the recovered memory about the abuse and the abductions.

She presented her subjects with a list of words such as "sugar" and "candy" and others. Then she removed the list and tested their recall. On the recall list, she listed some words that were not on the original list—words, for example, such as "sweet." "Sweet" puts the reader in mind of "candy" and "sugar," but it was not on the first list. Sure enough, a disproportionate number of people who reported recovered memories of sexual abuse and recovered memories of being abducted by aliens had high false-positive identifications of the words that were similar to words on the original list but that were not on it. These subjects rang up much higher false positives than those in the control groups.

> ### LESSON FROM THE STREET #44
>
> Empathy is shaped by circumstance and context. You have to focus and block distractions if you want to be empathic.

The context and feelings generated by looking at the similar words, Clancy concluded, created the memory—a representation from imagination, feelings transforming fiction into fact, the power of context.[8]

You think this overstates the power of suggestion created by context? Listen to this.

When Ronald Reagan was president he told a story to the then–prime minister of Israel, Yitzhak Shamir, that made the prime minister cry. President Reagan told about his experiences at the end of Word War II in the Signal Corps visiting death camps and recording the atrocities the Germans perpetrated. It was a poignant story. It contained a major flaw, however. Reagan spent his entire military service in Hollywood helping with the army film units. He had never been to the camps. But he had seen films of the atrocities, and, having seen them and having been so powerfully affected by them, he apparently convinced himself that he had been there. Perhaps it was because he was an actor, but when he saw the films about the death camps, our former president put himself in them.[9]

———

EMPATHY AND PRACTICE

That brings us to the essence of this chapter. That is, empathy and a high degree of skill in its exercise and application are learnable skills. As with most skills, practice is its mother. Some people may be more "naturally" empathic than others, but we have seen that across a wide range of possible qualities, factors within our control—and not genetic or gender determinants—are most important in developing this skill. Motivation, context, and practice—these are the major considerations.

Empathy, though, as we have said, is the exercised ability to infer what someone is thinking and feeling over a particular time frame and to act on that inference.

Now, some may quarrel with that definition because it is too cognitive or volitional. In other words, they can think of instances in which feelings of empathy arise automatically. You see someone peel an onion and begin to cry. You know, without thinking, how they feel. They have a point, but I'm not sure how useful that knowledge may be. What matters, it seems to me, is the volitional part: what do you do with what you know about the feelings of another.

STREET-SMART REALITY
THE DIFFERENCE BETWEEN APPEARANCE AND REALITY

Chris Katusky was my father's brother. My dad was a Katusky before he went to prison for bootlegging, came out, and changed his name to Smith. That's an interesting story in itself (and it does have something to do with dad's empathic accuracy about his family), but it's a story for another time. Uncle Chris had been injured at birth and, as result, had a severe speech impediment and was badly crippled, though he walked without assistance.

My sister and I lived with Uncle Chris and my grandmother for more than a year on a farm three miles outside Hayward, Wisconsin. In that time with Uncle Chris, my sister, Sandra, and I, ten and eleven, respectively, learned to stutter and to limp just like him. Sandra and I called him "Unka Chris."

Now, Sandra and I began imitating Uncle Chris's speech and walk to be funny at first—out of his sight, of course. Then, after we came to know what a remarkable guy he was, we began to imitate him to see if we could tell how he had felt as he lived his life. We would pretend we were crippled as we performed our chores. It wasn't easy. After some time, we thought we had a pretty good idea how he must feel limping around the farm doing his work, and soon, somewhat ashamed, we stopped imitating him.

Uncle Chris had no formal education. He'd never stepped foot in a school; but he was smart and could, as they say in Kentucky, spy where the egg was laid. He developed a thriving business in the sale to fishermen of small frogs they used as bait. He caught the frogs at a creek and in a pond on the farm, and he kept them and fed them at the bottom of an abandoned silo whose top was removed so the rain would blow in. Hundreds of the frogs lived on the cool and damp moss on the silo's floor. Sandra and I would creep into the barn quietly, stick our heads in the silo, and scream as loud as we could. The floor would erupt with jumping and croaking frogs.

One day, as we got off the school bus we could see Uncle Chris leading a group of fishermen toward the silo. Sandra and I ran to catch up with them. It was fun to catch the frogs and put them in a bucket, and sometimes Uncle Chris would give us each a quarter for helping him.

By the time we got to the silo, though, Uncle Chris was already climbing down the ladder to the bottom. He had a minnow bucket looped around one arm and he was descending with great difficulty. With about three rungs to go, he lost the bucket off his arm, and when he reached to catch it, he fell. He fell heavily and squashed about fifty frogs. His fall and the clattering bucket that skittered across the floor set up a real ruckus among the frogs, and one of the customers couldn't help laughing.

> **LESSON FROM THE STREET #45**
>
> Be careful what you assume about the feelings of others. "Walk a mile in their shoes" is not a myth; you actually have to do it.

"Unka Chris, I'll help you," I said as I crawled through the silo door and got one foot on the first rung.

Uncle Chris just sat where he had fallen, extended his right arm, and pointed his index finger at me.

"S-stay!"

I froze. Uncle Chris got up, netted up the three dozen frogs the fishermen had ordered, and climbed out of the silo.

For the rest of the day, we said nothing about what had happened, but at dinner I ventured a comment.

"Unka Chris, I know how you felt today at the silo." (I really thought I knew exactly how he felt.) "But those people didn't think anything about it, and, besides, we'll probably never see them again."

"No. You don't know how I feel. We'll probably never see them again, you're right. But I'll see my s-s-s-self," he stuttered, "m-m-m-many times in my mind falling down in that s-s-silo."

———

Does this mean you should practice being the person on the other side of the table as you bargain, the way Sandra and I "practiced" being Uncle Chris? Yes. It will make you more empathic. Exercise 2 offers a low-risk way for you to do this that will help you in your workplace persuasions.

THINKING ABOUT THE EXERCISE

What will playing these roles do for you? A number of things. First, you'll learn that there are probably some facts you don't know about the other side that you *should* know and, equally important, that you *can* know. You may identify a small piece of information that, if you knew it, may cause you to modify your presentation. Next, you'll get a good feel for your level of preparation. Are you well prepared or not so well prepared?

> **LESSON FROM THE STREET #46**
>
> To be empathic, practice. A small insight into the feelings of others can make a big difference.

Mostly, the exercise will help you practice being empathic. Few of us do this. And, as I hope this chapter demonstrates, practice is what is most important in developing empathy.

If you've read about Sherlock Holmes and seen, perhaps, the film about Holmes as a young man, you'll know that the younger Holmes was not nearly so sharp at reading people as the more mature Holmes was. The older Holmes gained his skills through years of practice.

Try the rehearsal a few times with a friend or a co-worker, and you will become convinced that it will help you be more empathic in your negotiations.

Pocketing the coin of empathy requires effort. But the rewards in *getting it* are abundant and overflowing—everybody benefits.

Exercise 2

THE REHEARSAL[10]

Let's pretend. Pretend you are the superstar in the drama of your own negotiation, a workplace negotiation you have coming up. Let's say you are at the theater the night before your play opens to rehearse an important scene involving you and your costar (the person with whom you will be negotiating). Time has passed, however, and your costar has not shown. You ask a stagehand to phone her. No answer.

What can you do?

The stagehand, an aspiring actor (and in real life this can be any adult), offers to help. You ponder. You are particularly interested in your costar's interpretation of her role and how she sees and relates to your character. And, of course, you wish to know more about her (the person you'll be across from in the upcoming negotiation).

You have an idea.

You ask the stagehand if he would play your role and you'll play your costar. He agrees but says he'll have to get some information about your character, the character of your costar, and the nature of the upcoming negotiation between the two of you in this important scene.

Time is short, but you are creative, so you set up the action this way:

First, you have the stagehand interview you about yourself (and/or, in real life, your company) and the issues between you and your costar (and/or, in real life, her company). Have the stagehand ask you questions such as the following. This should take about five minutes.

"Who are you and what is your upcoming conflict (negotiation) about?"

"Who is your costar's character (your opposite number with whom you will be negotiating), and where does he work, and what is his position?"

"Will other actors be present in the scene, and are there any ghosts at the table?"

"What are the issues between the two of you in this important scene (negotiation)?"

"What are your positions on the issues?"

continued...

The Rehearsal *cont'd*

"What is your desired outcome?"

"What are your hopes and fears about the resolution of the conflict (the negotiation)?"

"Have you had any people problems with the costar's character? What are they?"

"What will you do if you cannot in this scene (negotiation) resolve the issues between you?" (In other words, is there another character [company] with which you can make a deal?)

Now, the stagehand continues to gather information, but this time he gets the information from you as you play the role of your costar. He asks you (as the costar) questions such as the following. This should take about five minutes.

"What's your name and position?" (You respond with the costar character's name and job title.)

"How long have you been in your position?"

"Where did you work before?"

"Where did you go to school?"

"Are you a decision maker in your department?"

"Who are your key customers?"

"Who are your key competitors?"

"In the upcoming scene (negotiation), what is the star's character like?"

"What position will he take in the resolution of the issues in the upcoming scene (negotiation)?"

"What are his motivations (hopes and fears)?"

"What will he do if you cannot resolve issues (make a deal)?"

Finally, you are ready to play the scene. To gain the most from it, you, the star, continue to play the role of your truant costar. And the stagehand plays you. You go through the issues of your scene (your upcoming negotiation), taking care to stay in your roles and avoiding any conversation that is third person. For example, you would not say: "Well, I think he would be most afraid of not hitting the delivery schedule." Instead, you would say: "I am, among other matters, concerned about hitting our target dates for delivery." Playing the scene should take about ten minutes.

7

POCKET THE CURRENCY OF RAPPORT

The Tails Side of the Human Connection Coin

If you practice empathic accuracy, you'll learn about the thoughts and feelings of those with whom you are dealing. Armed with this information, you'll craft your requests from these good people and get them to comply with your wishes. They'll do this because you'll have a road map to rapport. Rapport, continuous rapport, is important in persuasion. It is the "tails" side of the human connection coin.

This word, though, requires a new definition if you are to get it in your daily efforts to persuade and negotiate.

If you consult your Funk and Wagnall's for a definition of *rapport,* you will learn that it is a positive connection in some, perhaps unspecified, way to another person. We need to expand that definition. For our purposes it is more useful to consider rapport to mean a connection to another person—positive, you would hope, or neutral, if not positive, but even slightly negative, if necessary. The connection—that's what's important.

Perhaps a better definition of rapport is the definition for another word that also looks different from the way it sounds. That word?

Rapprochement. This means to bring together. Connect. Glue. That's what rapport is. It sticks us together and keeps us there.

If you doubt the importance of connectivity in persuading people, consider this. In July 1999 the *New York Times* and CBS conducted a poll in which nearly 63 percent of those surveyed indicated that in dealing with other people you cannot be "too careful." More than a third—37 percent—agreed that "most people" will try to take advantage of you if they get a chance. But, and here is the encouraging news for you, 85 percent of those questioned said that if they knew the person "personally," such a person would be "fair" with them.

The Good . . .
the Neutral . . .
the Not So Good in Rapport

Rapport is a wonderfully elastic concept. It can be good, merely neutral, or even not so good and still create a connection—a kind of coactive connection—that will redound to your benefit with those you seek to persuade.

THE GOOD CONNECTION

Look again at the *New York Times*/CBS poll. It doesn't take much to be known "personally" and thereby qualify as someone who will be "fair."

STREET-SMART REALITY
LITTLE THINGS, BIG DIFFERENCES

Ann Stokes had been a successful businesswoman all her adult life. She had sold BabyTendas (a little table with a square cut out of the middle for the baby to sit in) and had been the company's national sales leader three years running. She had built up a regional nursing home company, sold it, and made a large profit. And along the way she had been president of the National Geriatric Society and vice president of the American Association of Nursing Homes. After she retired, her portrait was hung in the state capitol because of her pioneering efforts in the health care field.

So when her son started a fast-serve pasta restaurant, Pasta Pizzazz, she had the know-how and the motivation to help him. To begin with, she loved the restaurant. It was a former Kentucky Fried Chicken outlet that her son transformed into a sleek, modern structure serving specialty pasta dishes and gourmet pizza. Mrs. Stokes also felt a kinship with the enterprise because it served her state fair prize–winning carrot cake.

Business was excellent for a start-up, but since the restaurant was open from 10 a.m. to 11 p.m. seven days of the week, there were some very slow periods during the day. This created staffing problems as well as opportunity costs. The slow periods required a jump start.

One of the dead times was between 4 p.m. and 7 p.m. But Mrs. Stokes believed she had a solution for this time period. By the time the restaurant had started up, Ann had sold out of her health care company, retired, and was living about a mile from her son's new business. She had time and energy. She got a list from the voter registration people of everyone over sixty-five years of age who lived within two miles of Pasta Pizzazz and looked up every one of their telephone numbers. Then she began calling them.

> **LESSON FROM THE STREET #47**
>
> The connection you make, the rapport you build, may be only slight. That's all right. Little things can make a big difference.

"Hello, Mrs. Doris Ballantine? This is Ann Stokes and I am a neighbor of yours here in the Highlands—in fact, I live at 1412 Willow Avenue. You know the tall building by the Dartmouth? Well, that's the Willow Terrace, and that's where I live.

"I'm calling about my son. He's opened a new restaurant on Bardstown Road where the KFC used to be. Have you seen it? It's an unusual building with a lot of neon lights and interesting colors. The name is Pasta Pizzazz and he calls the design 'art deco.'

"Have you tried it yet? Well, you really should. The food is out of this world, and it is reasonable. And I don't know about you, but I am elderly, and I like to eat dinner early in the day. You do too? Well, it helps my digestion. I can't really eat after 7 in the evening or I pay for it.

"And, Doris, I want to encourage you to go to Pasta Pizzazz between 4:30 and 7, because they have an Early Bird Special that is about 30 percent cheaper than the same meal after 7 o'clock. And, get this: if you eat there four times you get your fifth meal free as a Frequent Diner!

"Here is my number and please call me 'Ann.' Once you eat there, please let me know about your experience."

After ten days, if she had not heard from Mrs. Ballantine, Ann would follow up with another call. The result? After four months of daily calling, revenue for the 4 to 7 p.m. period had grown to two and half times what it had been before Ann's calls.

Notice what happened here. A telemarketer was not cold-calling residents. A neighbor on behalf of her son was calling Mrs. Ballantine, a neighbor who, like her, was "elderly." And it wasn't far into the conversation that Mrs. Ballantine became "Doris" and Mrs. Stokes became "Ann." Thereby, Ann Stokes became known "personally" to Doris Ballantine, and, by the time she placed a follow-up call, Ann and Doris were friends. They liked each other. And Doris was then strongly disposed to try Pasta Pizzazz.

NATURAL ATTRACTIONS

When was the last time you were attracted to someone who didn't like you? Maybe in third grade. You'd hit little Tiffany on the arm as a sign of affection. She did not reciprocate, either the hit or the affection—unless you went to my grade school, St. Cecilia's, and her name was Ruby. If you hit her, she'd deck you, or her brother would.

But think about it. People you like usually like you. And if people like you they are predisposed, are they not, to do what you would like them to do? If this is a fact, and I think it is, then the key to establishing rapport with someone is to like them. Like them and they'll like you back. If they like you, the sky's the limit.

Dale, a heavy-equipment dealer, once asked Kentucky coal magnate Jim Smith why he used me to sell his coal. In a simple sentence Jim summed up the wide array of skill, ability, and knowledge about the coal business that I possessed at the time—in short, my usefulness in selling Jim's coal: "Because I like the hell out of him."

But maybe you don't like everybody. Jim surely didn't. Maybe you don't like many people. Or if you do like some people, you don't like something about them. So what is the key to liking people? There may be a number of keys, but the one that opens the most doors is this: You must like yourself to like other people. If you don't feel good about yourself, you're not going to feel good about those around you.

This isn't just a bunch of Freudian therababble. The fact is, if you feel good about yourself, then you can quiet your mind about yourself and focus on the persons across from you and find something about them to like. I learned about this self-comfort-leads-to-a-quiet-mind phenomenon playing tennis.

STREET-SMART REALITY
SELF-COMFORT AND THE QUIET MIND

A good tennis stroke, like a properly executed golf swing, is a thing of beauty. As you observe it, it seems to be seamless, integrated, all of one piece. But in fact it is complex and consists of many parts. When you're learning the game, it is hard to keep all the instructions in mind at once. Run quickly to the ball but swing deliberately. Swing low to high. Bend your knees. Watch the seams of the ball. Finish high. Let the torque of your body, not your arm, provide the power. Keep the face of your racquet perpendicular to the court surface.

Whoa! Think about all that at once and you'll hit the ball all right—over the fence or into the net.

I found that a better way to learn the game was to watch good strokes hit repeatedly and then just get on the court and try not to remember too much—maybe one thing, like swing low to high (so you can impart top-spin and help keep the ball in the court). I resisted letting my mind be like a bee, buzzing from one command to another. I said to myself, "Freeze the bee." Stop him in midair and just let your muscles remember what your eyes have seen without the interposition of your mind flitting from one instruction to another.[2]

I call freezing the bee the Quiet Mind Quotient® (QMQ®). Picking up the game in my midforties and with modest athletic ability, I was, by freezing the bee, playing tournament tennis in south Florida within a few years.

To test your QMQ, try this low-cost experiment. Find a co-worker with whom you have frequent policy disagreements and explain that you are attempting to improve productivity by turning policy debates into constructive plans for action. Get a video camera and lay out the ground rules.

For twenty minutes the two of you will discuss (debate) a current hot-button issue at work. Then, each of you will view the tape separately. You will view the tape first. At no fewer than four points in the twenty-minute discussion, you will pick out arguments your co-worker is making and you will stop the tape and write down what you think your co-worker was thinking and feeling at that particular time—not the obvious thoughts about marshalling the facts, but the feelings about what was going on between the two of you: what he or she was feeling about you and thinking about you and your reaction to what was being said. Then, your co-worker will view the tape and write down what he was actually thinking and feeling at those particular times. Sit together and compare notes.

Then, repeat the process with the co-worker privately stopping the tape at least four times and making notes about what you are thinking and feeling at those points. You review the tape and record what you were actually thinking and feeling at these points. Compare notes.

The comparisons will yield some very interesting divergences in opinion about thoughts and feelings as well as some convergences. You will begin to get a rough gauge at least of the kind of rapport you may have with this co-worker on this issue. Ask yourself, on a point where you missed what the other person was thinking or feeling, was it because of what you were feeling? In other words, did your emotional static get in the way of your accurately assessing the feelings of the co-worker and then connecting with her?

———

Have you ever had what you considered a great idea for your boss, but you think that you are probably not the right person to present it? This feeling could come from a variety of sources. For example, you don't have a reputation for the strong technical skill necessary to implement the idea, and your boss will likely discount what you say because of that. But whatever the reason, you're not the right person to present the idea. That's all right.

In fact, it is good that you recognize that you need another person to help you: You need a surrogate to make the right connection.

STREET-SMART REALITY
RAPPORT BY PROXY

It's lunchtime on Sunday. Let's go to Pasta Pizzazz and get some Alfredo. The restaurant is quiet. Only a few tables are occupied. Mrs. Stokes and her son are enjoying some carrot cake and coffee, and her son is reflecting on the curious unevenness of his business blessings.

"I just can't seem to get folks in here on Sunday until after 6 p.m. I could open later, say at 4 p.m., but there are some regulars who would complain. Plus, I think the more integrity you have in your hours, and the more you stay open, the more regular your customers will become."

"I've got an idea," Mrs. Stokes said, "and I'll get back to you tomorrow after I run it by a preacher."

A preacher?

The following day she laid out her proposal to build Sunday business.

"There are more than twenty churches within a mile of the restaurant. Let's give them a chance to generate some funds for their collection plates by offering to contribute 30 percent of everything a church member spends at Pasta Pizzazz between 12 p.m. and 5 p.m. on Sunday. We'll devise a simple identification /receipt system. Every week we'll remit directly to the pastor. Our costs, at least, will be covered. We'll build business. The 30 percent contribution is tax deductible. Everybody makes out."

After six months of the Sunday program, Pasta Pizzazz never again had a quiet lunch on Sunday afternoon.

Notice once more what happened. Mrs. Stokes created a positive connection with church members she didn't know through the person they did know and could be expected to feel good about, their minister. Rapport by proxy. Sometimes that's the best way to go.

> **LESSON FROM THE STREET #49**
>
> To build rapport, don't be afraid to use a proxy. It's the connection that counts.

———

THE NEUTRAL CONNECTION

If you can't develop what may be considered a positive connection with those you seek to influence, then develop a neutral connection.

STREET-SMART REALITY
A CONTACT, NEUTRAL, IF NOT POSITIVE

Benjamin Franklin, one of our founding fathers, was an expert at ingratiating himself with others. His *Autobiography* and the stories about him are rife with examples of how he got others to like him. But even if some didn't like him (and, like all great men, he had his detractors), he nonetheless would strive to make a connection of some kind with those whose influence he sought to curry.

One of his favorite techniques, after scanning the library of his host or hostess, was to ask to borrow one of their books. By this simple act he accomplished a number of "connections."

> **LESSON FROM THE STREET #50**
>
> Even a neutral connection can lead to influence-building rapport.

First, he implied that his host had read something he had not but that he wished to. This was flattering, since Franklin was regarded as well read, and his choosing a book at least implied that his host was a person of discriminating taste and wisdom. Second, by borrowing the book, Franklin placed himself in the debt of his host—he'd have to return the book—a posture of supplication in the view of some. Third, when he returned the book and by that gained favor with the owner, he had a chance to speak about the book and thereby deepen and broaden his rapport.

———

THE NEGATIVE

You may resist the idea, but even a negative connection may be better than none at all.

STREET-SMART REALITY
A NEGATIVE INTO A PLUS

A friend of mine from law school served in Vietnam, was captured by the Vietcong, and was held prisoner for several months. He was in isolation for long periods of time but was regularly tortured by two of his captors. Twice a week these same two men in black pajamas and flip-flops, and smelling of fish, would arrive at his cell and inflict pain on him in a variety of ways.

"After a few weeks, I could predict their arrival, and at first I dreaded the approach of the day and the time. But after several weeks of this treatment, the balance of my time spent in isolation, I began to look forward to their visit with a kind of perverse pleasure. Once when they didn't show up, I became—I know it's hard to believe—depressed."

My friend's experience is difficult for me to imagine, but while studying the fund-raising efforts of a worldwide organization, I remembered the story he told me and I began to understand what he meant. A human connection, even if it is negative, is still a human connection; and in the absence of much human contact, it may be better than nothing.

If you live in a city you may have seen them on the streets. I first saw them on Michigan Avenue in front of the Walgreens across from the Water Tower in Chicago. Dressed in saffron robes, heads shaven, dancing and chanting, shaking tambourines, and generally creating commotion, they formed a daunting gauntlet into the drugstore. They were members of a religious sect.

Willing to pay more to avoid them, I crossed the street and bought the more expensive shaving cream at Marshall Field's in the Water Tower. But as I crossed the street I noticed they had a guitar case open and apparently empty on the sidewalk in front of them. They were soliciting contributions. With no disrespect intended for their beliefs, I wondered how they could think the uncommon commotion they were causing would entice money from passersby. And apparently not very many passersby were so moved. Only a few coins rested on the bottom of the guitar case.

During the next few years I would see members of the group dancing, mostly jumping straight up and down, on my frequent visits to Chicago. Then they disappeared, and I wondered why. After I first became aware of them, I noticed stories about them in the press. They were, I read, building centers, building communities, and sponsoring all manner of projects. They had hundreds of affiliates (if that's the right word) all over the country. Where were they getting the money for all this? Not dressed in orange robes and bobbing in front of Walgreens. And where had they gone?

Reacting to cool customer response, they changed their fund-raising tactics. They carried little cases and they met you at the airport. They looked more like you and me, although not completely.

"Welcome to Chicago. Please accept this flower as a symbol of hospitality."

I didn't want a flower, but they backed up as I walked and kept holding it in front of me. Finally, so I could go on my way unimpeded, I took the flower. But the solicitor stayed with me, step for step.

"Sir, there is usually a donation for the flower."

"Well, I don't really need a flower, so, here, take it back and welcome someone else."

"No, it is yours to keep with or without a donation, but we would welcome a donation no matter the size."

"What's the usual size?"

"A dollar."

A dollar, I think, is a fairly inexpensive way to extricate myself from this situation, which, stripped to its bare reality, amounts to extortion. I hand over the dollar, take the flower, and then, slightly embarrassed, drop it in the next trash container. As I leave the airport, I see my benefactor's short-haired confederate picking flowers from the trash container outside the airport's pneumatic doors, gathering them for resale to the next target.

> **LESSON FROM THE STREET #51**
>
> Even a negative connection can build rapport if the connection is not too negative.

As I climb into my cab, I realize how the group is getting all its money: by selling flowers that most people throw away and then gathering them up and selling them again. There aren't many products you can sell and keep at the same time.

Some students of influence and persuasion would see these tactics as reciprocity at work. You get a flower. We get a dollar. Quid pro quo. Everybody is happy.[1]

That's not how I see it. Some donors, of course, may take their flowers and give them to their partners, passed off as thoughtful and considerate homecoming presents for the one who stayed behind. Those donors get value for their donation.

Most people, however, who give the money do so to extricate themselves with relatively little expense from an awkward situation. From a situation of negative connection or rapport. And maybe that is a quid pro quo of a kind. Note: the negative feelings generated from this exchange are not great enough to keep the group from raising millions of dollars in this, and other, uncomfortable ways.

————

Once you make a connection, once you establish rapport, there are a number of ways you can make that connection positive and continuous—ways to make it work for you.

Modeling . . .
Mirroring

Malcolm Gladwell observes in his book *The Tipping Point* that if you are happy you will smile and if you're sad you will frown. But, he says, if you are made to smile you will tend to become happy, and if you are made to frown you will tend to become sad. Emotion, in other words, goes inside out, but it also goes outside in.[3]

I had a friend, a great guy, a talented guy, who was not well educated and who spoke in the idiom of the streets where I grew up. He used the word "ideal" for "idea." He used the word "theys" for "there are" (as in, "Theys a lot of crooked politicians.") He wasn't handsome. He was 5'8", weighed 245 pounds, and had lost his left hand clowning around on a Ferris wheel. By his midthirties he also had lost most of his hair. But he was a great success with most women.

I asked one of them why.

"Riley always makes me laugh, and when he does it makes me happy," she said, smiling at the memory of him. She was predisposed to laugh at his stories. If she didn't feel good, Riley made her laugh and she felt better. Outside in.

MODELING

Try it. Smile at everyone you meet. It doesn't matter whether you know them, or whether you are in cool and aloof New York City or in friendly Enid, Oklahoma. You'll find that many folks will give you back a big smile, maybe a surprised smile, but a smile.

Said another way: You can model the feelings you wish to elicit in those around you. It's a variation of "monkey see, monkey do."

STREET-SMART REALITY
MONKEY SEE, MONKEY DO

I suspect that a lot of what we communicate to one another is not about the words we use. Maybe 20 percent is communicated via words and 80 percent via other factors: tone, timing, energy, emotion, body language, gestures.

My favorite speaker has a powerful effect on her audience. She is energetic. Her timing is flawless, her modulation dynamic. Her emotions ebb and flow. Her speeches are not paragons of logic. They frequently don't hang together. If you tried to repeat what she said in the order she said it, you'd have a hard time. But her audiences don't care. When you ask them afterward about her speech they say, "She really energized us!" They aren't sure what she said, but they want part of it. She was inspiring, energetic. Her message is her energy.

This modeling for results can be subtle but can have a big influence.

Brian Mullen of Syracuse University and a number of his colleagues in 1984 conducted a study that, for an academic work, has been widely reported and has created some controversy. It is worth looking at for its implications about influence exercised merely through facial expression—no words required.[4]

Mullen produced nearly forty 2.5-second videotape snapshots of Tom Brokaw (NBC), Dan Rather (CBS), and Peter Jennings (ABC) reporting on the presidential race between Ronald Reagan and Walter Mondale. The snapshots were without sound, and they were shown to groups of study participants who were, on the basis of what they saw, asked to rate the emotions of the broadcasters from negative to positive on a twenty-one-point scale. The continuum was from extremely negative to extremely positive.

Brokaw and Rather scored about the same when talking about Reagan and Mondale. But Jennings scored 13.38 when he talked about Mondale and 17.44 when he talked about Reagan—a 30 percent variance! The researchers concluded that Jennings showed a "bias in facial expression" in favor of Reagan.

Did this bias influence voters in the election? Professor Mullen and his associates called voters in a number of cities around the country and asked them how they had voted. In every instance, ABC viewers voted for Reagan in much greater numbers than those who watched CBS or NBC.

Now, it is possible, of course, that those who watched ABC were more predisposed to vote for Reagan anyway. But four years later Mullen repeated the study when Governor Michael Dukakis and Vice President George Bush ran against each other for president, and, again, Jennings rated more positive in his facial expressions when speaking about Bush than about Dukakis. Again, ABC viewers voted in higher numbers for the vice president.

What are the implications of this information for you in the workplace?

First, and this goes beyond the mere metaphor of "letting a smile be your umbrella on a rainy, rainy day," nonverbal communications are more powerful than you may believe. What you send out in your facial expressions, your body language, your gestures, and your tone will affect those around you and come back to you in roughly the same form. The higher you are in an organization, the more your modeling will be reflected in the attitudes and expressions of those around you.

> **LESSON FROM THE STREET #52**
>
> Follow the Get It! Golden Rule: Communicate unto others as you would have them communicate unto you.®

Second, some of these signals, sent perhaps without intent to be sneaky, are very subtle. You don't need to overdo them. Most people are not like my grandfather's mule. You don't have to hit them in the head with a 2x4 just to get their attention.

Keep a kind of inventory of your expressions at work—verbal and nonverbal. Practice, for example, varying your tone of voice and watch carefully the responses from your co-workers.

There are many ways you can say, just by varying your tone of voice, for example, "The Phoenix software initiative, if not implemented by December 1, will be off the table, and we will default to our present system indefinitely."

Notice, particularly if you have a number of reports (folks who report to you), whether they begin to mimic your tone, gestures, body language, and use of buzzwords. (Try this experiment: Say, "At the end of the day . . ." a number of times. Then notice how much your staff begins to pick up on that expression. Or, "Connect the dots . . ." or, "Do the math . . ." Soon you'll think you're attending a conclave for business clichés.) You'll be looking at your linguistic self refracted through the modeling of your subordinates.

When this phenomenon happens in the workplace, be certain it occurs because you want it to, not because it's an accident.

————

In persuasion, you build rapport by leading folks to model your expressions and behavior, and we've seen that this can be highly influential and convincing. You may build even stronger rapport and be much better at convincing if you are able to slip into the lives of others and likewise mirror what they do. Let them model for you, and then reflect what they do back to them. They can then see themselves (or who they would like to be) in you.

STREET–SMART REALITY
LINGUISTIC MIRRORING

Through the years we have learned from our students that each of us processes information in a particular way. Your particular way is the way you represent yourself to the world and the world to your self. Learn this about yourself and others and you have a road map to rapport.

You open the new product model for which your logistics company is going to provide fulfillment and distribution. It's a beautiful, stainless-steel serving cart with thick rubber wheels, three adjustable shelves, and a heavy-duty handle. In the picture on the box, that is. Out of the box, it is a jumble of trays, cylinders, wheels, and plastic attachment doodads. You have to "assemble it in eight easy steps."

Some people will study the instructions, which have been translated from the Chinese into English by a Korean in Hong Kong.

Others will ask a co-worker to read (and incidentally interpret) the instructions for them.

Still others will throw away the instructions and start putting the cart together without reading or listening to anything ("Let me get a feel for this: Should the wheels go on first or should I insert the cylinder in the top of the tray? Or is this 'top' really the bottom? Oh well, let's give it a shot. My gut says this is right.")

> **LESSON FROM THE STREET #53**
>
> See, hear, or feel—that's primarily how we experience the world.

There are, in other words, at least three dominant styles of processing information and, consequently, perceiving the world.

You see (read) it. You hear it. Or you feel it.

———

This does not mean that if you learn mainly by seeing or reading this is the only way you get information. It has been speculated, for example, that President Franklin Roosevelt may not have read a book after he graduated from Harvard. He got his information mainly by talking with people. But as president, surely he must have read a mountain of memos and documents he had to sign. Still, mostly he was a listener and a talker.

Like Roosevelt, you have a dominant style of processing information. You are visual, auditory, or kinesthetic. The words you use betray the dominant style you represent. By listening to word selections in ordinary speech you can determine other people's style, and, possessed of this knowledge, you can respond in kind. Through this verbal synchronicity you can build powerful rapport with those whom you would persuade. You can mirror them. And they'll like what they see because they will see themselves, or at least who they would like to be.

To understand the style of others, you must understand your own style. Exercise 3 will help you determine your dominant style. Are you a seer? A listener? A feeler?

Exercise 3

YOUR DOMINANT STYLE

To help you find your style, take this inventory. Put a checkmark beside the one of the three choices that best matches your reaction. There are no right answers. And don't try to be consistent.

In making business decisions, I

___ 👁 Study columns and rows of numbers on a spreadsheet

___ 👂 Bring in a group of co-workers to debate the issues

___ 🖐 Try a pilot project and get a sense for how it goes

When I have a problem at work, I

___ 👁 Write down a list of the reasons for the problem and a list of the possible solutions to it

___ 👂 Find someone I respect and talk it through

___ 🖐 Mull it over until I come to an intuitive conclusion about what to do

If a co-worker proposes an idea, I

___ 👁 Ask them to put it in writing

___ 👂 Ask them to explain it while I make notes or doodle

___ 🖐 Get a gut feeling about whether the idea will work

When I think of all the people I've known in my business career, the thing that impressed me about them most was

___ 👁 Their general appearance

___ 👂 The way they talked or a particular thing they said

___ 🖐 The way I felt about what they did

In making an important business presentation, I

___ 👁 Prefer to use flip charts, graphs, and other visual aids

___ 👂 Prefer a primarily verbal presentation so nothing will interfere
   with the power of the words

___ ✋ Prefer to demonstrate my point or how something will work

When my work requires some calculation, I

___ 👁 Tap it out on my computer, print it out, and study it

___ 👂 Whip out the mental math in my head if the problem is not too complex

___ ✋ Revert to my style in grade school and count up the numbers on
   my fingers

When I don't like a co-worker, I

___ 👁 Recoil when I see them

___ 👂 Recoil when I hear them

___ ✋ Recoil when I am near them

I know I am doing well at work when I

___ 👁 Visualize a new title on my office door

___ 👂 Hear my boss say, "Hey, great job. Keep it up and you'll get that raise!"

___ ✋ Get a promotion and a feeling of euphoria stays with me for days

I can become demotivated about a project at work if I

___ 👁 Cannot see where it leads or what is in it for me

___ 👂 Hear others bad-mouth the project with some good arguments

___ ✋ Imagine myself at the end of the project worse off than I am now

continues...

Exercise 3 *cont'd*

I can really get motivated on a new project at work if I

___ 👁 See clearly what to do and what a successful conclusion will look like

___ 👂 Tell myself and am told by others what a great opportunity this is

___ ✋ Imagine how great I'll feel when I accomplish my part of the task

Finding Your Score

To find your score, add up the eyes, ears, and hands icons. If the number is lopsided for one or another, that is your dominant style. If dominant for two, you're linguistically ambidextrous. Dominant for three? You're polydextrous.

Additional Steps in Understanding Your Style

To confirm your dominant style, pay attention to how you present yourself at work—what you say, how you say it, what you do. Does this empirical information confirm the inventory you have taken of yourself? If it does, you're in a good position to evaluate the styles of others. These evaluations will help you build continuous rapport.

Listen to what your co-workers say. At first, try to pick out those who are primarily visual. Then, look for the auditory and then the kinesthetic. If you try to do all three at once it is confusing, because you will not run into many who would score 10-0-0 in the above exercise. So focus on one at a time.

To help yourself, make a list of the words each style typically employs—especially the verbs.

For the visual, listen for every variant of the verb "see," for example, "look," "watch," "focus," "appear," "visualize," "mirror," "reflect," "illustrate," "show," and so on.

For the auditory, listen for every variant of the verb "hear," for example, "listen," "describe," "harmonize," "resonate," "tune," "tell," "speak," "shout," and so on.

For the kinesthetic, listen for every variant of the verb "feel," for example, "touch," "anger," "humiliate," "excite," "probe," "betray," and so on.

Make up your own list. Once you've developed a sense for this process, you're ready to build rapport by responding to those you would persuade in the language of their style.

SPEAKING THE LANGUAGE

When I first visited Spain to meet with the coal buyers from Cementos del Mar and other companies, my friend Crescente, a Chilean expatriate, went with me. He interpreted, because the cement company representatives, some of them, spoke limited English. At that point my Spanish consisted of only "Buenos dias" and "¿Que pasa?"

LESSON FROM THE STREET #54

Speak the language of those you would persuade and they'll be your new best friends.

The Spaniards were cordial, but half the time I wasn't sure we were really connecting. There was a lot of miscommunication. I decided that before I returned to Spain I would learn their language.

I bought tapes. I went to Berlitz. I hired a high school Spanish teacher who was a native of Mexico as a tutor. On my next trip I could speak some passable Spanish. I spoke Spanish from the time I got on the plane in New York City to depart for Madrid until I returned to New York.

The people in Spain were markedly friendlier to me. They were much more open in their dealings. They appreciated the fact that I was trying to learn their language. We were *simpatico. La lingua es muy importante para negotios.* Language is very important for business.

As it is in Spanish, so too it is in English. Most of us speak English, but our word selection reflects our information processing style, as we have seen. We will gain by speaking the language of those with whom we speak, trippingly on the tongue, if possible, as Hamlet said.

———

In the workplace, where buzzwords abound and clichés are king, it can be difficult to discern someone's linguistic style. Nearly everyone, for example, uses terms such as "bottom line," "incentivize," "downsize," "rightsize," "value added," "win-win," and on and on.

[STREET-SMART REALITY]
PERTINENT QUESTIONS, SYNCHRONICITY

The best way to knock aside all these verbal crutches so you can get at the style of the person you want to influence is to ask some pertinent questions.

I say "pertinent" because the question must relate to your interest in a particular issue. It can't just be "What kind of ice cream do you like?"

Are you trying to find out what makes someone buy something? Hire a consultant? Pass a zoning variance? Reduce the number of suppliers you have? Decentralize purchasing? The question should relate to the topic.

L. J. Green was a Lincolnesque purchasing agent for Air Products and Chemicals Company. He was always telling stories. I knew he would open up and reveal his linguistic style if I asked the right questions. I was trying to sell him coal.

"L. J., talk to me about some of your experiences in buying coal on the spot market."

"All right, Lacey. Let me *show* you something."

He handed me a two-page printed request for a proposal to supply stoker coal to the Air Products plant in Calvert City, Kentucky.

"When we *published* this in the papers, it wasn't two weeks and you never saw so many pin hookers in your life!

"I contacted my boss in Allentown, Pennsylvania, and I said, 'Lookie here, we can't spend our time trying to *clear* up all the questions these suppliers have about this RFP.

"Why, can't you *see* your way to let me just take a few of these suppliers who *appear* to be qualified out to the coal pile, *show* them coal we've got and how we burn it in the boiler?

"Let them *see* how it slags if it ain't the right size, and *show* what our operators have to do when that happens. If you let me do that, I'll *show* you an operator who will give us what we need."

L. J. was primarily a visual processor. His word choices made it obvious to me that to synchronize with him I should use the language of the visual. It was like being in Spain with the Spaniards.

LESSON FROM THE STREET #55

Ask the right questions to discover your new best friend's linguistic style.

I said something like this: "L. J., let me *see* if I understand *clearly* how you *look* at this. We've got all these words in the RFP to *look* at. And that's all right. But you just need for me to *inspect* the coal and *see* how it burns and say yes, I can give you coal that *looks* and burns just like what I *see* in the stockpile."

"Lacey, you've got it *clear* as can be."

Then I asked him a series of related questions that went something like this:

- "L. J. can you *show* me what your current supplier could do that would make you *look* at him in a different *light* so that you wouldn't be *looking* to change suppliers?"

- "Can you show me what you *saw* in him and his original proposal that made you pick him?"

- "Of all the folks who've come in here through the years, which one *showed* you the most for your money and why?"

His answers to these questions verified that he was primarily a visual processor of information. For me to maximize my success at building rapport with him, I had to use words that were consistent with his view of the world—through the sense of sight.

Some writers on mirroring maintain that those of us who display our distinct dominant visual, auditory, or kinesthetic processing systems also have correspondingly distinct breathing patterns, eye movements, gestures, and other nonverbal methods of communication.[5]

Some of these writers believe that by mirroring the nonverbal communication styles of others you can establish really powerful rapport with them. It is, they say, a matter of practice.[6]

Maybe.

STREET-SMART REALITY
MIRRORING AND MIMICRY

Where I come out on the nonverbal part of mirroring is where I came out trying to learn the "perfect" tennis stroke.

You can't remember everything, even if you're smarter than average. To calibrate, evaluate, and then act on and get feedback for your reactions to word usage, breathing, eye movement, and gestures, and other body language is too much to remember. Your mind would buzz like a hive of killer bees. To remember all this and act on it instantaneously, you'd have to be the best mime since Charlie Chaplin.

Instead, freeze the bee. Up your Quiet Mind Quotient. It's enough, in building rapport to focus on word usage as a clue to the styles of others, as a way for you to synchronize with them and build rapport. Plus, it can be risky to mirror nonverbal idiosyncrasies of others. Mirroring can quickly deteriorate into mimicry. At home when your preadolescent daughter repeats every word you say as you say it, you may, at least at first, be mildly amused. But in the workplace, mimicry can be disastrous.

Malachi worked for the consulting division of a large international financial services organization. In his dress, Malachi followed Shakespeare's advice that clothes oft proclaim the man. He was strictly Armani, Hugo Boss, and Gucci. On assignment for a Zurich-based insurance company, Malachi noticed that the CEO had a penchant for Gucci bridle-bit loafers. Malachi had a pair in black and a pair in cognac himself, and he began wearing them on the days he knew he would see the CEO. On one such day, while Malachi was "mirroring" the CEO by crossing his left leg as the insurance executive crossed his right and letting his Gucci dangle off his foot just like the executive, the CEO noticed Malachi's footwear.

> **LESSON FROM THE STREET #56**
>
> Don't try to mirror nonverbal communications. It's too risky. Mirroring can become mimicry, phony and easy to spot.

"Hey, I thought I was the only one around here who wore Gucci," he said without the trace of a smile on his face or in his voice.

Malachi ditched the loafers and went back to lace-up Cole Haans for the rest of the assignment. He also stopped mimicking the CEO.

———

It's better to slip into the world of others by using their words—words that betray how they perceive the world—words that are visual, auditory, or kinesthetic.

Practice this kind of mirroring, and you'll develop all the continuous rapport you may ever need. This rapport will be your tails side of the human connection coin.

8

BAKE A BIGGER PIE TO GET A BIGGER PIECE

Building on the Differences Among the Parties

"Make the pie bigger." You hear people say that a lot. The expression is a cliché, like "thinking outside the box." As we have seen, however, a cliché is a cliché because it expresses a truth so aptly that people wear it out with overuse. They don't try to think of a better way to say the same thing.

It is true that when you consider dividing up a pie, if you can make it bigger, you have a chance to get a bigger piece for yourself. But for this expression to be useful as you persuade others, we have to import some specific meaning into it.

First, No Pie . . .
Then, a Bigger Pie

Paradoxically, before thinking about what making a bigger pie means, you should first consider not having any pie at all. Consider what will happen, that is, what you will do if you don't persuade those whom you would influence, if you can't make a deal. What is your no-deal alternative? You have to think about no deal before you can think productively about making a better deal.

STREET-SMART REALITY
NO PIE AND YOUR BATNA

If you can't make a deal, will you get up from the bargaining table, go to the door, and look out into a kind of existential abyss, and, unable to return, make a leap of faith into the blackness? Or do you have a place to go? Have you identified your Best Alternative To a Negotiated Agreement? Your BATNA?[1]

What is the best you can do if you must walk out the door? It is important that you distinguish among your various alternatives and single out the best one. Remember, "best" is a superlative word. There's only one. Do that and then you know what kind of deal you have to make at the table where you're sitting. It has to be better than your BATNA. If it's not, you walk.

In addition to giving you a benchmark against which to measure your progress in persuasion, identifying your BATNA also gives you the confidence that you don't have to make a deal in your current negotiation. This confidence is power.

Billy Ray Beckett had worked on a deal for his company for nearly six months. It was going to be his ticket to a promotion and a raise. All he had to do was negotiate a basis point yield that met the hurdle rate he and his boss had established as the minimum target. That done, he was golden. He and his fiancée could set the date, buy the house, and get on with it.

As with most of life, though, Billy Ray had a challenge. He preferred to call it a problem. His company had agreed to loan $100,000,000 to a French auto parts maker. Billy Ray had persuaded his boss to originate and service the loan, keep $15,000,000 in their portfolio and sell off $85,000,000 in participations to other firms. Billy Ray's company had sequestered its money, and Billy Ray had lined up the participants.

His challenge, or more properly, challenges were these: First, in negotiating with the French representatives, at critical points, they lost their ability to speak English, especially when the conversation turned to interest rates, basis point yield. Second, the French were represented by a New York investment banker who was a graduate of the "nuke-'em-til-they-glow" school of negotiation. He was truculent, rude, and, so far, intransigent on the all-important issue of interest rates.

Just back from a frustrating meeting in New York, Billy Ray, who had been one of my MBA students, called me and we discussed his situation.

"Billy Ray, tell me, when is your next meeting?"

"In ten days."

"What will you do if you don't make the deal?"

"I have to make it. I've worked on it for six months. My promotion, my raise, my marriage—just about everything depends on it."

"Yes, but what if you don't make the deal, what are you going to do with your $15 million and the money your participants have put up?"

"Lacey, you aren't listening. I've got to make this deal."

"What is the percentage chance that you'll make the deal—99 percent?"

"No, it's more like 99.9 percent!"

"Well, let's look at that one tenth of one percent. You have to figure out where you'll put that money—yours and your participants'—and what your basis point yield will be if you can't make the deal. In other words, you have to determine what your Best Alternative to a Negotiated Agreement with the French auto maker is. Figure out what you're going to do with that money and call me before you leave for New York."

> **LESSON FROM THE STREET #57**
>
> Before trying to make the pie bigger, consider what you'll do if you have no pie at all.

A full week later, Billy Ray called. He had found a place to park all the money if the auto parts deal fell apart. The yield was somewhat less than his target with the French. But finding that parking space gave him time to find another, perhaps better, deal.

"How do you feel now, B.R.B.?"

"Better. A lot better."

"Call me when you get back from New York and good luck."

Billy Ray didn't wait. He called me from New York.

"Lacey, it happened just as I thought it would. The French could speak no English at crucial times. The 'I' banker got so mad, he left the hotel conference room and went back to his office. But I didn't panic. I knew what I had in my back pocket, my BATNA, so I adopted my 'Bo Peep' strategy."

"What's that?"

"I left them alone, knowing they would eventually come home, wagging their tails behind them. And they did. Faced with my silence and my willingness to sit there for what seemed like hours, the French polished their English. The 'I' banker (who by the way had a multimillion-dollar fee at stake) regained his civility and came back to the hotel. And we made a deal. A deal at a higher yield than my target."

"Great!"

"And that's not all. My boss is ecstatic. I get the raise and the promotion. I get to go to Paris to close the deal, and I get to take my fiancée with me!"

————

Billy Ray had a strong BATNA, and during the course of the negotiation with the auto maker and the investment banker, he chose not to reveal anything about his alternative. At least he didn't reveal it overtly. But his Bo Peep strategy probably indicated to them that theirs was not the only game in town.

STRONG BATNA

If you have a good BATNA, should you reveal it to your opposers? It depends on how you do it. You have to be both believable and tactful. If you are not believable, they'll conclude you're lying, that you actually have a weak BATNA, and bargain with you accordingly. If you aren't tactful, they may be offended and break off the negotiations. You have to strike a balance.

If you choose to reveal your BATNA, use a light touch: "John, we are eager to make a deal with you. We have, as you probably know—it's not possible to keep a secret in our business, is it?—been approached by HardDrive Systems. They've put an attractive offer on the table, but I want you to know that we strongly believe you are a better fit for us in both the mid- and the long term; and we very much hope we can partner with you."

Merely a glimpse at your weapon, a passing reference to a possible deal with another company. That's all you need to communicate the power of your BATNA.

When you have a weak BATNA the considerations are somewhat different.

WEAK BATNA

You've done your best to identify alternatives, and the best you can come up with is none too good. This happens. If you are a health insurance company operating in a market where there is only one neurosurgeon, negotiating with this service monopolist puts a premium on creativity as you bargain over the prices he will charge your policy holders for his exclusive procedures. You have nowhere else to go and he knows it.

Still, except in situations such as this hypothetical, there are tactics you can employ to mitigate what appears to be a lack of bargaining power suggested by a weak BATNA.

STREET-SMART REALITY
A WEAK BATNA AND ITS EFFECT ON BARGAINING

Sally is an opera star but an aging one with hopes of a comeback.[2] She had not sung a lead in two years and her salary for secondary roles during that time ranged from $10,000 to $18,000. Her prospects for a career rebirth had been dim when fate presented her with an opportunity. The Lyric Opera has a performance of *Norma* opening in two weeks, and its soprano has a medical condition which will prevent her from performing. The soprano was to be paid $30,000 for the run of the show.

Sally's agent and the opera business manager will try to negotiate a deal. Sally has told her agent that she would be willing to sing for next to nothing just to have the lead because it could produce offers for lead roles again and television shows. The board of the opera has authorized their representative to offer Sally up to $45,000. If they can't get Sally, they will hire the understudy soprano whom they can get for less than the $30,000 they had contracted for with the original lead singer. The understudy, however, is an unknown quantity. The opera's board is concerned that people may not show up without a name singer in the title role. This could produce a big loss, and their primary interest is to avoid such a loss.

Put yourself in the shoes of the Sally's agent. What is your BATNA if you can't get at least an industry standard amount for Sally? Have her sing for nothing? You won't do that for a variety of reasons, not the least of which is that if she gets nothing, you probably get nothing. Also, in the small world of the opera, word gets around; and if Sally sings for nothing or next to nothing this will set a bad precedent for her future. And yours.

In the shoes of the opera business agent, things aren't much brighter. His BATNA is to go with the understudy. But this is big risk given the fear the board has for a financial loss. Sally was a big star at one point, and she knows she has you over a barrel with the show beginning in two weeks. What if she won't go for the $45,000?

Weak BATNAs all around. Do they affect bargaining performance? Absolutely. Should they? Absolutely not.

LESSON FROM THE STREET #59

If your BATNA's weak, don't show it. The other side may not know.

In the case of Sally and the Lyric, although each side has much of the same information, there is some information known only to one side or the other. The business manager does not know how motivated Sally may be to sing the lead. And Sally's agent, though he may guess as much, does not know the full range of the Lyric's alternatives. For all he knows, the business agent could be negotiating with Kiri Te Kanawa as well as with Sally.

What do you do with a weak BATNA?. In the first place, recognize it. Then, try to affect both your perception and the other side's perception of it.

How can you at once recognize the weakness of your BATNA and at the same time try to change your view of it? Follow the advice of the song. Instead of being gripped by fear, "whistle a happy tune so no one will suspect" you're afraid. Put on your party face. And know that if you practice this enough, it will affect how you feel. Remember: Emotions go inside out, but they also go outside in.

With respect to the other side's perception of your BATNA, just because your BATNA is in fact weak, the other side may not guess that. So don't let them know. Don't lie. ("Sally is considering a very attractive offer that will consume all her time beginning the first of the month.") But this is a good time not to blab the truth. (A better approach: "As you may know we have been weighing Sally's options. She has considered retirement, and this is popular with her family but not with her many fans. So she is considering some other possibilities. What you are offering will be one among several. It is, of course, very short notice—even though Sally is, as you know, entirely familiar with the role and could probably get in costume and perform this afternoon.")

Once you have fully considered your no-pie possibility, you are ready to make the pie bigger.

Most negotiators think of their problem as dividing up whatever it is that is at issue among the parties. Money, time, resources—human and others. They think that if the other side gets something, then they lose something. They think, in other words, that the pie is of fixed size.

It is true, of course, that no matter how big the pie gets, at some point it will be divvied up. And someone will get a bigger piece than someone else. Pure equality of outcomes rarely exists in the business world, and therein lies the illusion behind the expression "win-win." The expression suggests that with a win-win solution everyone ends up about the same. This is almost never the case. It's like the animals in Orwell's *Animal Farm*: All the animals were created equal but some were more equal than others.[3]

It is useful to look at the purely distributive aspect of dividing the pie before focusing on expanding it.

DISTRIBUTIVE NEGOTIATION

Let's go back to Steve Thompson, the fish farm, and his negotiation with Alvin, the Chicago entrepreneur.

Steve had a minimum that he would accept for the farm, and Alvin had a maximum that he would pay. Each also had a target price that he would like to achieve in a best-case scenario.

Expressed graphically and in thousands of dollars, the Bargaining Continuum (BC) may have looked like this:

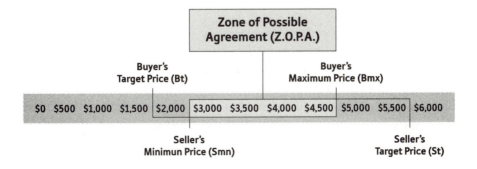

The BC for Alvin and Steve indicates that while the target of each is unacceptable to the other, there is an area between the minimum Steve would accept (Smn) and the maximum Alvin would pay (Bmx) where a deal could be made. This is the Zone Of Possible Agreement (ZOPA)[4] along the BC. In this case, however, in bargaining strictly over money, Steve and Alvin didn't make a deal, though clearly they could have.

This happens. Not because the result is rational. An impasse is reached where a deal may not be made because of the emotions of the parties: stubbornness, face-saving, ego, and the like.

When agreements are reached in cases like these, the point of agreement is only one of many possible within the ZOPA along the BC. Steve and Alvin could have made a deal anywhere between $3 million and $4.5 million. But as long as they insisted on their targets, there was no way to get into the ZOPA.

INTEGRATIVE NEGOTIATION

An agreement was possible, even given their positional bargaining, if they had looked beyond the boundaries of their conflict.

STREET-SMART REALITY
RESOURCES BEYOND THE BATTLEFIELD

Nearly every negotiation involves more that just a single issue. Money is the dominant issue in most business negotiations, but usually there are others. Look for them.

Let's construct a hypothetical that could have helped Steve.

Hundreds of miles from the Mississippi fish farm, let's say Steve had an additional problem. Among Steve's responsibilities was the Jack Daniels Distillery in Lynchburg, Tennessee, which produced a by-product of the distillate process that was a clear liquid and 99 percent protein. The company practice had been to pump this liquid into catchment basins where it evaporated. The residue, after a rain, was absorbed by the earth. Company engineers opined that this practice was completely benign to the environment. The Federal Environmental Protection Agency was not so sure.

Recently, a team of engineers from the EPA district office in Atlanta visited Lynchburg and as a result sent a letter to the company headquarters in Louisville, asking that the company drill several 5,000-foot water monitoring wells around the distillery and submit periodic reports to the EPA evaluating water quality on several criteria. If the company were forced to do this, it would be costly and time-consuming.

The EPA had become a stone in Steve's shoe as he ran around the country trying to sell the fish farm, itself an increasingly daunting task.

Steve, before entering the spirits business, had a career in the food business. Among other companies, he had worked for Hunt Foods. Reflecting on his experience, and against the backdrop of his training as an engineer, he had an epiphany. Since feeding the fish is a major cost of operating a fish farm, and since fish eat protein, why not pelletize the protein causing him a problem in Tennessee and make it available to any potential buyer as food for the fish in Mississippi?

Acting on this epiphany, Steve accomplishes a number of things.

He improves his BATNA of going to court with the EPA or, depending on the comparative cost, acceding to their request to drill wells, either alternative very costly. His new BATNA is to collect and pelletize the liquid and sell it (not so costly).

> **LESSON FROM THE STREET #60**
>
> Look for resources beyond the immediate conflict. Bring them to the table to expand the pie.

Plus, by turning this liability into a resource not at the table in negotiations over the fish farm, Steve makes moving along the Bargaining Continuum into the ZOPA with Alvin a real possibility.

Does this lemons-to-lemonade scenario have a kind of deus ex machina quality? Like the U.S. Cavalry saving the settlers from certain death or like the cancer of the judge who wanted a case to be settled?

It's not so far-fetched. Steve's epiphany about the liquid protein brings resources to the bargaining table not previously present—resources beyond the battlefield, the conflict—and these resources make the pie bigger. They greatly expand the ZOPA. Expanding the ZOPA is often possible; you just have to look for ways to do it.

Another way to expand the pie is to explore the different priorities each party assigns to the various issues in a negotiation. Then, trade on the issues that are comparatively unimportant to you, but may be important to the other side. And insist on advancing your full set of interests on those issues that are of paramount importance to you. These issues may not have as high a priority for those on the other side of the table.

STREET-SMART REALITY
DIFFERENT STROKES FOR DIFFERENT FOLKS

Return for a moment to considerations of the aging opera singer, Sally. We looked at her situation and that of the opera from the perspective of their BATNA's, what they'll do if they can't make a deal. Think now about the various interests of each party. Sally is mainly interested in a leading role and a comeback. The opera is mainly interested in avoiding a big financial loss. Money is more important to the opera than to Sally. Because of their comparative difference in priority on this issue a number of possibilities present themselves.

Sally could sing for very little money and agree to some nonmonetary compensation. She could be given an elaborate dressing room with fresh flowers every night. She could be permanently featured on promotions that the opera is going to produce anyway. If she sings for little, of course, she runs the risk of setting a precedent, not only with this house but in the business; and that could be self-defeating.

> **LESSON FROM THE STREET #61**
>
> People value things differently. Trade on these differences to make the pie bigger.

To overcome this potential problem, Sally could agree to be paid an annuity with a low up-front cost but paying in the future at least what a top soprano would be paid, although not in today's dollars. She could couple this annuity with a confidentiality provision in her contract prohibiting disclosure of what she was paid and how. This way the opera would avoid the big investment that could, if the house is not filled, lead to a big loss. Sally, with a deal like this, could assert that she had received top dollar for her performance.

Sally is confident that she still has star quality and can fill the house. The opera is not so sure. One way to trade on the different assessment each attaches to this issue is to peg Sally's compensation entirely to her performance. She gets a low or no base and every dollar she is paid is keyed to house occupancy, how many seats she fills.

Different parties, different interests. As Sly and the Family Stone sang in 1969 at Woodstock, "Different strokes for different folks."[5]

———————

Another way to look beyond your current issues or conflict, as Steve looked beyond his Tennessee problem to a solution in Mississippi, is to try to compensate the other side, if not on this deal, on some other contemporaneous or future deal.

I'm talking about a variant of the "take-care-of-me-on-this-and-I'll-take-care-of-you-on-that" way to make the pie bigger.

STREET–SMART REALITY
NOT ON THIS DEAL BUT ON ANOTHER

LogisticTek is a logistics company that does a lot of business with Electronics, a large conglomerate in the electronics field, with sales in the scores of billions of dollars. Electronics is the classic 800-pound gorilla insofar as its suppliers are concerned. It does pretty much what it wants, sits where it wants, and pays suppliers what it wants to pay them. If that doesn't suit, it gets a new supplier. Take it or leave it. When their relationship began years ago, LogisticTek merely stored Electronics' appliances and shipped them out pursuant to their customers' orders. In time, however, LogisticTek evolved into a supplier that had a multifaceted relationship with this giant company. LogisticTek stores and ships product. It removes the skin from many of the appliances and fabricates stainless steel coverings. It receives and evaluates damaged products and determines whether a particular item should be repaired, sent to a scratch-and-dent re-seller, junked, or merely re-packaged and returned to the plant because the packing box but not the appliance was damaged.

Each year the LogisticTek board chairman meets with the head Electronics purchasing agent to negotiate its contract to apply stainless to its appliances. Each year the agent asks LogisticTek to reduce its price to Electronics. Most years these negotiations result in no change in the contracts, but in a recent year, Ron, the agent, insisted on a 6 percent reduction. A concession of that size would almost wipe out LogisticTek's margin. The parties went back and forth, and at length Ron confided that he had to get a concession of that size or the company was considering bringing the fabrication work in-house. Frank, LogisticTek's chairman, didn't want to lose the business but didn't want to do it for nothing either.

> **LESSON FROM THE STREET #62**
>
> If you can't expand the pie at the table where you're sitting, look for an issue on another deal where you can make a trade.

After a good bit of too-ing and fro-ing, Frank asked Ron, "Isn't there some additional work we could do for you so we could make up a little on this lost margin?"

"Well, we could have you start electronically testing the scratch and dent items we send you. We have to pay our people to test them as it is, and our fully loaded hourly cost for that work is almost $65. Are you interested?"

Frank was interested and the deal they made on testing the scratch and dent business produced enough profit to make a price reduction on the stainless business acceptable.

What, you may ask, is different about what Frank and Ron did and what Sally and the opera did? Sally and the opera could trade issues *within* the conflict or negotiation at the table. Ron and Frank brought into the conflict over the stainless business an issue from an entirely different deal, different contract, even a different department in Electonics. They brought in an issue from *outside* the conflict over the stainless business. In this way, they found another way to make the pie bigger.

———

Another way to expand the pie is for one party to get exactly what they want (usually money or some form of it, like time), and then the second party's concessions are made less onerous because the first party helps the second cut its costs.

STREET-SMART REALITY
TRADING AND ITS MANY FORMS

Remember Toya in Chapter Three, who was mandated to negotiate with a sister company without knowing the full nature of the corporate relationships between and among the American and Japanese companies? In a world of many choices, the ownership relationship between the companies created a sole-source situation for Toya. But she was creative. Using her company's substantial leverage in purchasing, she helped cut the cost of the sister company; and she was able, thereby, to reduce the price her company had to pay for the components the sister company supplied.

In this situation, a potential impasse is avoided, not because Toya changed her position or compromised her interests, but because she helped the sister company making the concessions feel no pain—something the sister supplier could not accomplish alone.

> ### LESSON FROM THE STREET #63
>
> If an issue is cost, many times one party can lower the price it pays by helping the other party lower its costs. The pie, thereby, grows.

The success of this pie-expanding tactic obviously depends on a number of circumstances. The two parties must share information. In Toya's case, she needed to know the cost structure of the components she was buying, where the component parts were purchased, the transportation cost, and so on. Only the sister company could supply this to Toya. Sharing is not always possible, but when it is, powerful integration—pie building—can take place. Taking away the pain of giving up something in a deal often also depends on an economic disparity between the parties. A huge company, as in this case, can buy things more cheaply than a small one.

————

The positions parties take, we have seen, are not the same as the interests which underlie these positions. If the underlying interests can be clearly identified, it is often possible to span the gap between the parties' opposing positions and, thereby, expand the pie.

STREET-SMART REALITY
CONFLICT OVER THE KIWIQUAT

The kiwiquat is a fruit found in scant quantities in the jungles of sub-Sahara Africa.[6] The fruit has long been believed to contain powerful medicinal qualities, but until recently the consensus of the medical community has been that most of these qualities reposed mainly in the minds of certain tribal medicine men.

As is often the case with medical research, two teams have been working with the fruit in parallel but unrelated projects. Until recently neither team, at Research Labs or Drug Corporation, was aware of the work of the other. But circumstances have arisen that have brought the teams' activities to light. This knowledge, along with the scarcity of the fruit, has produced conflict between the companies.

The Research Labs team has extracted a serum from the juice of the kiwi-quat, a foul-smelling nectar, that has shown phenomenal results in treating HIV/AIDS, and if the drug can be put into immediate production, thousands, maybe millions, of lives may be saved that would otherwise be lost to AIDS.

The Drug Corporation team has likewise been working hard, and it has discovered from oil contained in the hairy skin of the fruit a chemical that produces a vapor that, when injected into the trigger mechanism of weapons of mass destruction, renders the mechanism completely inoperative. It turns the weapon into a dud. This vapor is urgently needed to save thousands of lives.

The issue that has arisen between the companies is that Chief Jessie Omugme, head of a major Rwanda tribe, has 5,000 kiwiquats—all of last year's production—and he knows he's got every kiwiquat on the face of the earth.

Knowing better than to get in a bidding war against each other, the Research Labs and Drug Corporation teams have been negotiating for three weeks over how to divide up the fruit before they approach Chief Omugme. Each company needs all 5,000 kiwiquats. The two companies have a history of bad blood between them, and several lawsuits involving them are at various stages in state and federal courts. Their negotiations over the kiwiquats, therefore, resemble those of two black widow spiders preparing to mate. They are proceeding very carefully, and so far negotiations are at an impasse.

> **LESSON FROM THE STREET #64**
>
> Find out what the parties really want. Differences may provide rich opportunities to expand the pie.

Why at an impasse? After all, they need different things. One needs the juice and the other needs the skin. Why not, together, just make the best deal they can with Omugme, and then take the part each needs?

The answer contains the explanation to why most negotiations, where there are interests markedly different from the parties' positions, break down. People take a position and dig in. Listen to the Research Labs and Drug Corporation negotiators.

"We need the kiwiquats."

"All of them?"

"Yes, all 5,000."

"Well, so do we. We need them all."

"If we can get all 5,000 and soon, we can save thousands of people from certain death by AIDS."

"Hey, if we can get all 5,000 we can possibly save the world from chemical weapons in the hands of terrorists!"

And so it goes.

To span the gap between their positions, the negotiators need to meet each other as problem solvers and not mirror reflections of their warring companies. They need to exercise empathic accuracy and build rapport. They need to ask each other ever more probing questions to find what their real underlying interests in the kiwiquat may be. If they do this skillfully, in time they well discover that they need different things from this rare fruit.

––––––

The negotiation between Research Labs and Drug Corporation illustrates the importance of sharing information between the parties to build on the differences among the divergent underlying interests. The question is "How much should you share?" If you spill your guts in an effort to get the other side to do likewise and they don't spill theirs, how much of a disadvantage does that put you at?

Margaret Neale, a professor at Stanford University, calls this sharing of information "opening the kimono." You don't want to show too much or too little. To do it right, you've got to strike a balance. You have to share enough that you elicit the information you need from the other side but not so much that they can then crush you with the knowledge they gain from what you say or from what you show them.

My prescriptive advice is to share information candidly on issues that have the lowest priority for you but be parsimonious with information on those issues that are of greatest priority. To test whether the other side is doing the same thing, ask them, after they share information, just how important that issue is for them.

STREET-SMART REALITY
AFTER THE DEAL, A BETTER DEAL

Howard Raiffa, a professor emeritus at the Harvard Business School, suggests that perhaps parties can make better deals if, after they have reached an agreement, they further agree to share all their information to see if this can produce a better deal for at least one party without worsening the deal for the other: a kind of post-deal deal.[7]

This is an intriguing suggestion for making the pie bigger. But it's a risky suggestion.

Once all the information is out on the table, the other side may have a bad reaction to what you had not previously disclosed; and they may regret, perhaps with some bitterness, the deal they have made—even if the new information permits them to make a better deal. If you have future dealings with these parties, those negotiations may be adversely affected by what happened as a result of these disclosures.

> **LESSON FROM THE STREET #65**
>
> Sharing all the information after you have reached a settlement seems like a good way to make the pie bigger. But it's risky. Somebody may get mad.

Raiffa further suggests that one way to avoid this risk is to have a third party evaluate the shared information and suggest, without revealing the total sum of the information to either party, a way to make a better deal than the parties have made without full disclosure. This may work but could be cumbersome, costly, and contains some risk of undesirable disclosure.

———

Look for ways to bake a bigger pie in your persuasions. There are a lot of ways to do this. Explore them all as a matter of practice, and you maximize your chances to make a deal.

GET IT? GOT IT? GOOD!

The Most Memorable Lessons from the Street

We live on the top floor of a building whose front windows look out on the biggest baseball bat in the world. Twelve stories tall and weighing 68,000 pounds, the bat is a replica of Babe Ruth's Louisville Slugger that hammered out so many home runs in the 1920s. Made of wood-grained carbon steel, the sculpture sticks up, a surprise, in the city skyline and leans at 11.5 degrees off center, nonchalant, against the Hillerich and Bradsby building, where the real bats are still carefully crafted for the boys of summer.

If our building were as tall as the big bat, we could look south and see another city icon, a giant bottle of Old Forester bourbon whiskey, a spirit sentinel, at attention, 218 feet above the Brown-Forman Corporation's offices. Topped off with the product that bears its name, the replica could fill 800,000 pint bottles. Somewhat farther south, we could see the twin spires of Churchill Downs, home of the fabled Kentucky Derby, and not far from there is Yum! Brands, corporate headquarters for Kentucky Fried Chicken, Pizza Hut, Taco Bell, Long John Silver's, and A&W.

Sports, spirits, and fast food. Maybe that's how the world sees us. But soon Louisville, Kentucky, will also be known for what this book is all about: street-smart negotiation.

From the deck at the other end of our home, Barbara and I can look out on the Ohio River and watch the construction of a monument to another Louisville symbol and icon, Muhammad Ali, subject of the book appropriately titled *Greatest of All Time.* This 93,000-square-foot project, the Muhammad Ali Center, will be more than a museum. With its mission "to preserve and share the legacy and ideals of Muhammad Ali, to promote respect, hope, and understanding, and to inspire adults and children everywhere to be as great as they can be," it will also be a center to promote, among other public service goals, peace and conflict resolution.

Muhammad Ali grew up in the streets of Louisville's west end—the same streets I ran a few years before him—and it will be altogether fitting when some of the lessons he learned from the street are used to reduce conflict in Ali Center programs sponsored in his name, lessons like the ones in this book.

Of the sixty-five lessons from the street I have included in the previous chapters, five are particularly important. If you remember these—even if you forget the other sixty—you have an excellent chance to *GET IT!*

The Hopes and Fears Lesson . . .
It's Not About Numbers and Analysis

At any particular time, there are more than 1,000 books in print in English on the subjects of negotiation and persuasion—getting people to do what you want them to do. With few exceptions, the authors argue that the key to effective persuasion is to put emotions aside, ignore them, or control them, much as you might treat a cold or a fever.

My experience—personal and professional—tells me that the contour of almost every persuasion is shaped by emotions: hopes and fears.[1] It's not about logic and rationality. Your task is to understand your emotions and those on the other side, because these emotions define our interests as we perceive them. Your goal in every attempt to persuade as you try to *get it* is to advance your full set of interests and to satisfy the other's side in a way that is at least acceptable to them. This means dealing squarely with the emotions of everyone involved.

The Powerful Question Lesson . . .
That's an Interesting Price
(or Term, or Time, or Condition).
Where Did You Get It?

Ask this probing question, not as a challenge or a taunt, but as a sincere effort to get information about the interests on the other side. (In other words, you say in effect, "That's an interesting price, and its size doesn't run me off, and if you can show me that what we are bargaining over is worth that price—and if I can afford it—I have an open mind. I am persuadable.")[2]

You will know you have effectively asked this question when you in turn ask yourself this auditing question, "Do I know what hopes and fears have shaped the positions the other side is taking?"

If you understand these hopes and fears, then you will know how to frame your proposal to the other side so there is a maximum likelihood that the folks on that side of the bargaining table will agree to what you want.

If you do not understand these underlying hopes and fears, you will find that your efforts to persuade will be positional. You—both sides—will shout at each other about what you will and won't do across an ever-widening aperture of misunderstanding.

The Mythical Construct Lesson . . .
the Pie to Be Cut Up Is Fixed in Its Size

Our experience with the pies we eat tells us they have a finite size, and no matter how many pieces you divide them into, one eater can eat more pieces only at the expense of another eater.[3] The metaphor, however, does not extend to the pie of benefits that constitute what we bargain over.

In almost every situation there are ways to make these pies bigger. If you consistently and habitually look for ways beyond those that immediately suggest themselves as solutions to the issues between parties (e.g., "What do you say we split the difference?"), you will practice making the pie bigger.

A seller wishes to sell his house in tough economic times. A buyer wants to buy the house, but her credit is insufficient to support a loan. Does the deal collapse? Not necessarily. Perhaps the buyer and seller can enter an agreement—a contract for a deed—in which the seller will get his price and the buyer can make payments toward that price while living there. They bypass the traditional ways of making a sale and at the same time satisfy each other's interests. A bigger pie.

If you find yourself in a stalemate over an issue, ask yourself this auditing question, Am I assuming that some feature of a proposal is bad for me just because it is good for the other side? If you answer yes, then you are assuming the pie is fixed and that if the other side gets a piece, it's a piece lost to you.

The Level of Events Lesson . . . "By Their Deeds Ye Shall Know Them"

The honeyed words of a slick talker are seductive. We've all been taken in by the oily charlatan from time to time.

Try to operate on the level of events.[4] Go by what happens, not by what is said. This doesn't mean that what is said is unimportant. It is indeed important. Consider spoken words to be hypotheses you test against the actions of the speaker. See if the actions match the words—no excuses, no rationalizations. Did he do what he said he would do? And please know that you are likely to be judged by the same standard.

The Empathy and Rapport Lesson . . . Empathy and Rapport Form the Two-Sided Coin of Human Connection

Rapport will permit you to uncover the hopes and fears governing those on the other side. Genuine empathy for the feelings of others is of immeasurable help in building rapport.[5] When you practice empathic accuracy, you open the door to a powerful rapport with another, and in that state you will learn all you need to know to frame any proposal you may need the other side to agree on. These matters cannot be faked. Your empathy has to be authentic. "I feel your pain" is not sufficient. But even a slight rapport can make a big difference in outcome.

These are the five lessons above all to remember. If you will grapple these lessons to your memory with hoops of steel (to borrow from Shakespeare), you'll get it; you'll have got it; and that will be good—good for your company but also good for you and those around you! And, really, isn't that what *getting it* is all about?

If you need to jog your memory about any of the sixty-five lessons from the street, this list will help.

Street-Smart Lessons to Get It!

- **Lesson 1.** Hope frees you from fear.

- **Lesson 2.** In persuasion, keep your hopes high. You won't do better than your highest hopes.

- **Lesson 3.** What's "fair" most often determines who gets what, and what's fair is often not logical.

- **Lesson 4.** Sometimes people won't do what's good for them if they think it is "too" good for you.

- **Lesson 5.** Don't assume your perception of what is good for others is their perception. They may have different information, different emotions.

- **Lesson 6.** People are motivated more by fear of loss than by the hope for gain.

- **Lesson 7.** If there are at least two reasons for everything—the one you give and the real reason—don't fool yourself. Know the difference.

- **Lesson 8.** Focus on the problems of the other guy. You'll go a long way toward solving yours.

- **Lesson 9.** Don't be afraid to ask a question that creates an awkward silence. Ask an elliptical question and see what happens.

- **Lesson 10.** In communication, there's no such thing as too much clarification.

- **Lesson 11.** To deal with a negative, try raising it up front with a well-phrased question that anticipates the objection but is affirming at the same time.

- **Lesson 12.** "That's an interesting price—where did you get it?" is one of the most powerful questions you can ask. Ask it; then listen.

- **Lesson 13.** Body language and third-party information can help uncover interests, but be skeptical of information gleaned only from these sources. Don't be afraid to rely on your gut feelings.

- **Lesson 14.** Action mobilizes you and overcomes the paralysis fear can produce.

- **Lesson 15.** Someone without too much information can often provide a fresh look, a new insight, a different approach.

- **Lesson 16.** People on the other side are concerned about something. What is it?

- **Lesson 17.** Listen to experts, but don't let them lull your disquietude. No one cares as much about your interests as you do.

- **Lesson 18.** Don't be extravagant with displays of what you know. That almost never helps you get what you want.

- **Lesson 19.** Anger is something to expect in ourselves and in others, so get ready for it.

- **Lesson 20.** When someone is angry, let them get it out. Then say, "Well . . ."; then let them get the rest out. Don't debate. Deflate.

- **Lesson 21.** Be an anger detective. Find out who is mad at whom.

- **Lesson 22.** If you prepare better than the other side does, you'll do better nine times out of ten.

- **Lesson 23.** Don't lowball, thinking you can always go up later. There may not be a later.

- **Lesson 24.** Make a fair offer and your credibility goes up.

- **Lesson 25.** When time to prepare is tight, remember: Issues, Positions, Interests.

- **Lesson 26.** If you don't identify the ghosts at the table, they'll come back to haunt you.

- **Lesson 27.** Where should you negotiate? Where most of the parties are most comfortable.

- **Lesson 28.** When should you negotiate? Usually the answer is "Do it now."

- **Lesson 29.** Don't split the difference just because it seems fair. The result should get you where you want to go.

- **Lesson 30.** Except for your partner, don't fall in love with just one thing. Have a Plan B.

- **Lesson 31.** Without give and take, nothing would ever get done.

- **Lesson 32.** Don't confuse tactics and ethics.

- **Lesson 33.** When you sidestep the truth, even for a good cause, be prepared to pay a price.

- **Lesson 34.** Don't lie, but don't blab the truth either.

- **Lesson 35.** Don't rely on words. Operate on the level of events. Verify with tactful questions.

- **Lesson 36.** The power to commit yourself gives you the power to convince and persuade.

- **Lesson 37.** Get it in writing and you've got a prayer. Get strong constituencies to support it and you've got a deal.

- **Lesson 38.** Feeling the same emotion as another, or at least recognizing it, is the beginning of empathy.

- **Lesson 39.** Empathy has many faces. You may share someone's emotion and not his feelings.

- **Lesson 40.** Accurate empathy requires clarification. Check to make sure you understand what you see and hear and that you have been understood.

- **Lesson 41.** Empathic accuracy is important. But even if you miss the mark, you can still get an "A" for effort.

- **Lesson 42.** People give off signs and signals about their feelings. Some are innate, some volitional. Practice distinguishing them.

- **Lesson 43.** Women are more empathic than men but mainly because they want to be.

- **Lesson 44.** Empathy is shaped by circumstance and context. You have to focus and block distractions if you want to be empathic.

- **Lesson 45.** Be careful what you assume about the feelings of others. "Walk a mile in their shoes" is not a myth; you actually have to do it.

- **Lesson 46.** To be empathic, practice. A small insight into the feelings of others can make a big difference.

- **Lesson 47.** The connection you make, the rapport you build, may be only slight. That's all right. Little things can make a big difference.

- **Lesson 48.** To build rapport, focus. Freeze the bee. Up your Quiet Mind Quotient®.

- **Lesson 49.** To build rapport, don't be afraid to use a proxy. It's the connection that counts.

- **Lesson 50.** Even a neutral connection can lead to influence-building rapport.

- **Lesson 51.** Even a negative connection can build rapport if the connection is not too negative.

- **Lesson 52.** Follow the Get It! Golden Rule: Communicate unto others as you would have them communicate unto you.®

- **Lesson 53.** See, hear, or feel—that's primarily how we experience the world.

- **Lesson 54.** Speak the language of those you would persuade and they'll be your new best friends.

- **Lesson 55.** Ask the right questions to discover your new best friend's linguistic style.

- **Lesson 56.** Don't try to mirror nonverbal communications. It's too risky. Mirroring can become mimicry, phony and easy to spot.

- **Lesson 57.** Before trying to make the pie bigger, consider what you'll do if you have no pie at all.

- **Lesson 58.** When you have a strong BATNA, don't hit them over the head with it.

- **Lesson 59.** If your BATNA's weak, don't show it. The other side may not know.

- **Lesson 60.** Look for resources beyond the immediate conflict. Bring them to the table to expand the pie.

- **Lesson 61.** People value things differently. Trade on these differences to make the pie bigger.

- **Lesson 62.** If you can't expand the pie at the table where you are sitting, look for an issue on another deal where you can make a trade.

- **Lesson 63.** If an issue is cost, many times one party can lower the price it pays by helping the other side lower its costs. The pie, thereby, grows.

- **Lesson 64.** Find out what the parties really want. Differences may provide rich opportunities to expand the pie.

- **Lesson 65.** Sharing all the information after you've reached a settlement seems like a good way to make the pie bigger. But it's risky. Somebody may get mad.

NOTES

Chapter 1. Get What You Want

1. Antonio Damasio, *Looking for Spinoza* (San Diego, CA: Harcourt, 2003).
2. North Carolina Senator Edwards expressed the theme of hope above cynicism repeatedly in his 2004 bid for the presidency of the United States.
3. Karen Horney, *Neurosis and Human Growth: The Struggle Toward Self-Realization* (New York: Norton, 1950).
4. This statement was frequently quoted after Namath's New York Jets defeated the highly favored Baltimore Colts in the 1969 Super Bowl.
5. Daniel Kahneman and Amos Tversky, "Judgment Under Uncertainty: Heuristics and Biases," *Science* 185 (1974), 1124–1131; *Choices, Values, and Frames* (Cambridge: Cambridge University Press, 2000).
6. Ludwig Von Mises, *Human Action* (New Haven: Yale University Press, 1949).

Chapter 2. Uncover Emotions to Reveal Real Interests

1. *Jerry Maguire* (1996) was produced by TriStar and directed by Cameron Crowe.
2. *All the President's Men* (1976) was produced by Warner Brothers and directed by Alan J. Pakula.

3. From Hardee's national advertising run in April and May of 2003. Interview by the author on June 23, 2004, with Bev P. Harms, director of public relations, Hardee's.

Chapter 3. Discover Emotions That Betray You

1. Antonio Damasio, *The Feeling of What Happens* (San Diego, CA: Harcourt, 1999).
2. *Chicago* (2002) was produced by Miramar and directed by Rob Marshall.
3. William Shakespeare, *Othello,* Act V, Scene II, Line 348.
4. David Maraniss, in an interview by the author, June 10, 2003, confirmed the story that appeared in his book *The Clinton Enigma* (New York: Simon & Schuster, 1998), p. 23.
5. Norm Sherman, Sen. Hubert H. Humphrey's press secretary, interview by the author, June 19, 2003; also confirmed in an interview with Bill Connell, Sen. Humphrey's chief of staff, who worked with the senator since the mid-fifties, June 10, 2003.

Chapter 4. Prepare to Get It!

1. Rudyard Kipling, "The Elephant's Child," in *Just So Verses* (London: Smith, Elder & Co., 1898).
2. This hypothetical is derived in part from a negotiating seminar held at Harvard Law School, June 1984, Roger Fisher instructor.

Chapter 5. Prepare Some More to Get It!

1. William Shakespeare, *Macbeth,* Act I, Scene V, Line 62.
2. Interview by the author, Princeton University, Woodrow Wilson School of Public and International Affairs, 1963.
3. Example from Roger Fisher, a lecture, Harvard Law School, 1985.

Chapter 6. Pocket the Currency of Empathy

1. *Diner* (1982) was produced by Warner Brothers and directed by Barry Levinson.

2. P. J. Devries, "Enhancement of Symbiosis Between Butterfly Caterpillars and Ants by Vibrational Communication," *Science* 248 (June 1990), 1104–1106; P. J. Devries, "Singing Caterpillars, Ants, and Symbiosis," *Scientific American* 267 (October 1992), 76–82.

3. Charles Darwin, *Expression of Emotions in Humans and Animals* (London: J. Murray, 1872).

4. Compare E. Hatfield et al., *Emotional Contagion* (Cambridge: Cambridge University Press, 1994), and William Ickes, ed., *Empathic Accuracy* (New York: Guilford Press, 1997).

5. Deborah Tannen, *You Just Don't Understand: Women and Men in Conversation* (New York: Ballentine, 1990).

6. R. Rosenthal and B. De Paulo, "Sex Differences in Eavesdropping on Nonverbal Clues," *Journal of Personality and Social Psychology* 68 (1979), 854–869.

7. John Darley and C. D. Batson, "From Jerusalem to Jericho: A Study of Situational and Dispositional Variables in Helping Behavior," *Journal of Personality and Social Psychology* 27 (1973), 100–119.

8. Susan Clancy et al., "False Recognition in Women Reporting Memories of Sexual Abuse," *Psychological Science* 11, no. 1 (January 2000), 26–31; Susan Clancy et al., "Memory Distortion in People Reporting Abduction by Aliens," *Journal of Abnormal Psychology* 111, no. 3 (2002), 462–470.

9. Michael Korda, "Prompting the President," *The New Yorker,* October 6, 1997.

10. The rehearsal exercise echoes portion of a curriculum created for the Harvard Negotiation Project by Andrew Clarkson with the help of Phil MacArthur, copyright 1988, 1989, 1990 by the President and Fellows of Harvard College. All rights reserved.

Chapter 7. Pocket the Currency of Rapport

1. W. Timothy Gallwey, *The Inner Game of Tennis* (New York: Random House, 1974).

2. Robert Cialdini, *Influence* (New York: Quill, 1984).

3. Malcolm Gladwell, *The Tipping Point* (New York: Little, Brown, 2000).

4. Brian Mullen et al., "Newscasters' Facial Expressions and Voting Behavior of Views: Can a Smile Elect a President?" *Journal of Personality and Social Psychology* 51 (1986), 291–295.

5. Michael Brooks, *Instant Rapport* (New York: Warner Books, 1989).

6. M. LaFrance "Posture Mirroring and Rapport," in M. Davis, ed., *Interaction Rhythms: Periodicity in Communicative Behavior* (New York: Human Science Press, 1982), 279–298.

Chapter 8. Bake a Bigger Pie to Get a Bigger Piece

1. Roger Fisher and William Ury, *Getting to Yes* (Boston: Houghton Mifflin, 1981).

2. The facts of this example are from a Harvard Negotiation Project case study, "Sally Swansong," by Norbert Jacker and Mark Gordon.

3. George Orwell *Animal Farm* (New York: Harcourt Brace, 1945).

4. I first encountered this acronym in David Lax and J. K. Sebinius, *The Manager as Negotiator* (New York: Free Press, 1986).

5. Sylvester "Sly" Stone Stewart, "Everyday People," Daly City Music, 1968.

6. This fact pattern follows closely an exercise that is part of General Electric University's executive training program.

7. Howard Raiffa, *The Art and Science of Negotiation* (Cambridge, Mass.: Harvard University Press, 1982).

Get It? Got It? Good!

1. See Chapter 1 for a discussion of hopes and fears.

2. See pages 28–30 for a discussion of this question.

3. See Chapter 8 for a discussion of the bigger pie.

4. See pages 88–90 for a discussion of operating on the level of events.

5. See Chapters 6 and 7 for discussions of empathy and rapport.

INDEX

AUTHOR CONTACT INFORMATION

Lacey T. Smith
711 West Main Street
Louisville, Kentucky 40202
502-639-5064
laceysmith@quickthinkseminars.com